Adaptability, self-esteem, and learned helplessness in
connection to alcohol consumption

FEBRUARY, 2011

ACKNOWLEDGEMENTS

"Fear of the Lord is the beginning of knowledge".
"He that is humble, ever shall have God to be his guide".

What better can a statement be to express my earnest gratitude to all those who have helped me carry out the present endeavour- they all were angels personified, to guide, motivate and contribute to my humble being's efforts.

"Giving birth and nourishing, having, yet not possessing", working yet not taking credit, leading without controlling or dominating. Each word of the above stands to it's ultimate truth while I refer my supervisor Dr. Harprit Kaur. A learned, assiduous and persevering guide whose avid interest in process of my research has mentored me to see through the project, has left me deeply indebted to her. But for her able guidance this work would still be in my dreams.

I genuinely extend an ocean of thanks to the faculty and teachers at Psychology Department especially Dr. Sangeeta Trama (Professor and Head, Department of Psychology) who took keen interest in fulfillment of this research project. All of them untiredly responded to my nagging queries with frank opinions and critical comments which at the end proved monumental in shaping up this work to it's present level of academic value.

My bouquet of thanks goes to the administrative and clerical unit of Psychology Department who generously helped me in carrying out my work.

I am eternally indebted to my husband Dr. Gyanendra Pratap Singh for his support and assistance in carrying out this dream of mine. Without him being in my life it would not have even possible to conceive of such effort of pursuing research at this stage of life where one has unending personal, family and social responsibilities. My beloved sons Cyril and Yuvraj, little angels are yet another motivation, inspiration and a big boost for me.

And most importantly all my research Subjects whose trust on me and the work, I am doing has humbled me as a person. I from deep core of my heart extend my heartiest gratitude to them.

A special word of thanks to Mr. Rajiv Sharma (Director, British School of Languages, Moga) for his help in proof reading and editing the final draft.

I will be failing in my duty if I do not place on record my gratitude to the almighty God for blessing me with the strength and wisdom to pursue my research work.

Usha

6

CONTENTS

LIST OF TABLES

LIST OF FIGURES

INTRODUCTION

Man has been experimenting for thousands of years with a variety of naturally occurring substances that act on his nervous tissues. In ancient times alcohol was used by royal families or kings, just to get the freshness of mind and pleasure. But the poor used the drugs in the natural form (Bhang, Opium and Nicotine etc.). Thus the problem of alcoholics and drug addiction is not new in the history of mankind. In India although fermented alcohol "Somras", bhang, opium have been in use for a long time, the use of synthetic or chemical drugs relatively new. The menace of drug abuse is not only spreading alarmingly in urban areas, but also in rural areas and targets young adult population.

Drug abuse and alcoholism is widely recognized as a serious problem world over with severe psychological, social and physical consequences. Hence the problem of drug and alcohol abuse is not unique either to India or to present times (Sachene, 1990) but is a chronic menace.

The health care system is greatly affected by alcoholism. In India, 10% of adults entering private physician's clinics are alcoholics and 15-40% of adult admissions to general hospitals are for alcohol related problems. (W.H.A. Report, 2002). One fact comes to the forefront while analyzing the whole scenario that is what makes certain drinkers strictly remain social drinkers while others further deteriorate to drinking as a habit and become addicts/dependents.

11

Alcohol abuse affects not only the individual users but also their families and the general community. The harm can be physical, psychological or social in nature. The abusers pose difficult problems for themselves, for families, for industrial and other establishments and society.

DSM IV-TR (A.P.A., 2005) differentiates different levels of alcohol use as follows: -

Alcohol dependence is characterised by at least three of specific signs or symptoms from inability to control the amount consumed interferences with work, school or social activities, tolerance, withdrawal and duration of problem being at least for a month.

Problem drinker: These are people who can not drink in a controlled manner, or people whose drinking at one time has adversely affected their health or caused them any economic, professional, legal or personal problems (National Institute on Alcohol Abuse & Alcoholism, 1992).

Social drinking: can be defined as drinking pattern that is found to be acceptable to the society in which they occurs on an infrequent basis during social occasions that may call for alcohol to be present and/or consumed. Those individuals who engage in social drinking generally only have one or two drinks and are easily able to stop drinking at that time. Social drinking is defined as such because under normal circumstances, the individual would probably not choose to consume alcohol but may do so only due to the social situation (United State Department of Health and Human Services, 1992).

Alcoholism poses a significant threat to affected individuals, their families and the larger community. Understanding those variables that are involved in the etiology and maintenance of alcoholism is thus a high priority for both the clinicians who treat alcoholics and public health workers attempting to prevent alcohol dependence and related problems. Although a number of biological, psychological and social factors have been implicated in the etiology of alcoholism (National Institute on Alcohol Abuse and alcoholism, 1997), the general belief is that personality plays an important role in causing alcoholism.

Over the past 50 years, hundreds of studies have examined the personality correlates of alcoholics, many of these in search of so-called "Alcoholic Personality" (Sutherland & Tordella, 1950) that was thought to underlie alcoholic behavior. In the first edition of the American Psychiatric Association (APA, 1952), alcoholism was considered a form of personality disorder, implying that disordered personality functioning is a core component of alcoholism.

By the year 1980's, the alcohol research committee came to recognize that, although there was no single constellation of personality traits that was unique to alcoholics, personality measures could be used to distinguish clinical alcoholics(i.e. individual seeking treatment for alcoholism or individual meeting diagnostic criteria for alcoholism) from various comparison groups.

PHASES IN THE DEVELOPMENT OF ALCOHOLISM

Studies of the effect of alcohol show that it functions physically as a depressant and its most important psychological effect in easing of tension and fear. While there is no uniform pattern in the psychological and social development of alcoholism, some common stages have been identified. Jellinek, (1960) have describe a pre alcoholic phase in which the future alcoholic attempt to alleviate everyday tensions of life by drinking. At this point he is not considered to have a drinking problem. However, as he consumes progressively larger amount of alcohol in order to gain the same effect that less alcohol used to give, the drinker imperceptibly slips from the pre-alcoholic to the to **the phase of early alcoholism.** The early alcoholic may experience blackouts, brief periods of amnesia during or immediately following a drinking episode. He begins sneaking drinks and actually hides a bottle to drink from when no one is looking. He gradually develops a pre occupation with alcohol and experiences guilt about his drinking behaviour.

During the **phase of loss of control** the drinker loses the ability to abstain even for short periods of time. If he takes one drink, he continues to the point of drunkenness. This has been called **crucial phase** because during it the alcoholic stands in great danger of loosing everything he values (family, job, friends, health). At this stage

14

he may show tendencies toward grandiosity and intensified aggressiveness toward others. During the fourth and final phase, the **chronic phase**, the individual goes on prolonged, unplanned drinking spress (benders) which last for many days. To get money for liquor he may steal and write worthless cheques. Some female alcoholics resort to prostitution. During the chronic phase, the alcoholic's thinking become impaired and he experiences a loss of alcohol tolerance. When this happens he requires relatively little alcohol to arrive at a severely intoxicated state.

CAUSES OF ALCOHOLISM

Biological causes:

There may be a metabolic defect in the individuals physiologically who are dependent upon alcohol. Alcoholics have reported to metabolize at a faster rate than non-alcoholics. The genetic factors are also probably involved in the development of alcoholism in man.

Socio cultural causes:

The facilitating effects of certain cultural factors on the development of alcoholism is well recognized. The value and mores of the community in which an individual lives influence his drinking behavior. Occupation appears to be an important causal factor in alcoholism. Working in the drink trade itself wine merchant places the individual at a high risk but others including printers, businessman or doctors tend to manifest high rates of alcoholism. Predisposing effects include the availability of cheap of free alcohol, strong peer pressure to drink, a lack of supervision at work etc. Alcoholism has been reported to develop during periods of crises or following significant life events which have led to serious instability, confusion and role stress. It seems reasonable to hold that the presence of alcoholism in a marital partner might by itself constitute a sufficient incentive to divorce or separation.

Psychological causes:

According to psychological view, alcoholism, like any other deviant behavior or symptom, is the result of maladaptive learning and must be corrected by a process of retraining. According to psychoanalytic view, (Fromm & Maccoby, 1970) concluded that heavy drinking by men is a response to a repressed, intense mother fixation. From a psychoanalytic view point, alcohol can be considered to be substitute for emotionally mature adaptation, as a result of variety of specific failures in emotional growth. The alcoholic is seen as an economically and emotionally dependent person, passive and lacking in perseverance, devoid of interest in achieving anything other than immediate pleasure or relief. His love relationship is characterised by a self centeredness, a clinging to mothering persons and depressive moods when such support is not forthcoming.

According to the behavioral theories excessive drinking has been suggested by Bandura (1969). According to him, Individuals who are subjected to stressful situations may obtain relief from stress through

16

drinking alcohol due to its pharmacological effects. The behavior of drinking is reinforced by the reduction of unpleasant experiences that follows from it. Repeated experiences in which the drinking of alcohol leads to a reduction of anxiety, stress or other aversive stimuli results in a progressive strengthening of the alcohol habits. Once established, the excessive use of alcohol begins to have aversive effects on the individual that in turn set up renewed stimulus conditions for continued drinking. Eventually, with prolonged heavy drinking, physiological alternations occur in the body resulting in physiological dependence. Other behavioral factors may have etiological significance, however, social reinforcement, such as peer approval, or imitative behavior, e. g. of parental drinking attitudes and habits, may serve to initiate and/or maintain excessive drinking.

According to the personality theories, it involves the fact that alcohol act as a potent tranquillizers for highly anxious individuals. There is support for the view that some alcoholics manifest high level of anxiety and that alcohol has depressant and sedative pharmacological properties. Another view suggests that alcoholics are individuals who suffer from pervasive feeling of inferiority which result in an enhanced need for power in the face of inadequate personality resources to achieve it. Owing to frustrated ambition, the alcoholic resorts to drinking to achieve a sense of self-satisfaction and achievement as well as a release from tension.

The hazardous and harmful use of alcohol has now become one of the most important risk factors to health; and ranks third in developed countries. According to the (World Health Report, 2002), While alcohol use is deeply embedded in many societies, recent years have seen changes in drinking patterns across the globe wherein rates of consumption are in excess among general population, and heavy episodic drinking among adult people are on the rise. Alcohol consumption contribute to a wide range of diseases, health conditions and high risk behaviors ranging from mental disorders and road traffic injuries to liver diseases and unsafe sexual behavior.

Psychologically, etiology of substance abuse is believed to be a predisposition related to severe ego impairment and disturbances in the concept of self (Leigh, 1985). The person retains a highly dependent nature, with characteristics of poor impulse control, low frustration tolerance and low self-esteem (Jones, 1959). Described these persons as fixated at the oral stage of development and as ones who seek satisfaction through oral gratification (i.e. ingestion of substances). Having once experienced the gratification of supportive, drug induced pattern of ego functioning, users attempt to repeat this satisfying experience as a solution to their conflicts (Milkman & Frosch, 1980).

Research suggests that certain personality factors/traits may play an important role in both the development and maintenance of alcohol dependence (Barnes, 1980). Characteristics that have been

18

identified include impulsivity, negative self concept, weak ego, low social conformity, neuroticism and introversion. It has also been associated with antisocial personality and depressive response styles (Leigh, 1985). This may be explained by the inability of an individual with antisocial personality to anticipate the aversive consequences of his or her behavior. It is likely that in an effort on the part of that person to manage negative emotional evaluations, he may indulge in substance abuse. Further it may be an impulsive act towards anxiety relief. Achievement of relief then provides the positive reinforcement to continue abusing the substance.

Factors within an individual's culture help to establish patterns of substance use by modeling and through social attitudes; cultural acceptance and availability of substance are also highly significant. For centuries, French and Italians have considered wine an essential part of the family meal. The incidence of alcohol dependency in them is low, and acute intoxication from alcohol is not common. However the possibility of chronic physiological effects associated with lifelong alcohol consumption cannot be ignored. Historically, a high incidence of alcohol dependency has existed with in the Native American Culture (Westermeyer & Baker, 1986). Approximately 70% of adult in USA drink alcohol, of which 10% are heavy drinkers and 5 to 10% are problem drinkers (Frances & Franklin et al, 1994). Thus ethnic cultural influences are marked in the levels of alcohol use. Different investigators have given definitions of personality:

"Internal, organized, and characteristic of an individual over time and situations....[and] has motivational and adaptive significance" (Watson, Clark & Harkness, 1994).

Personality: the underlying causes within the person of individual behavior and experience.

Allport (1937): "the dynamic organization within the individual of those psychosocial systems that determine his unique adjustment to the environment."

Cattell (1950): "personality is that which permits a prediction of what a person will do in a given situation"

PERSONALITY AND ALCOHOLISM

Costa & Mc Crae, (1992) found that personality and alcoholism can be spuriously related because of "third variable" causation. For example, throughout the adult years, alcoholism is more prevalent among males than among females. However many personality variables are related to gender.

Besides from spurious relations, research on personality and alcoholism has suggested several models relating personality to alcohol use and abuse.

First, there are those models that posit personality as a predisposing factor. In these models, personality traits are thought to lead to alcoholism for any of a number of reasons. Personality traits could provide the primary motivational basis for alcohol consumption (eg. Negative affects regulation sensation seeking). Alternatively,

20

personality traits could affect the likelihood that an individual who is already drinking is likely to continue drinking despite the fact that alcohol is interfering with his or her life.(eg. deficits in inhibitory control). Yet a third possibility is that personality traits contribute to the development of specific alcohol related consequences (eg. alcohol related aggression) in someone who has consumed alcohol (eg. in individuals high in trait aggressiveness).

HARDINESS

Hardiness is a newer area of personality. After reviewing the literature, it has been found that few studies have done by different researchers on hardiness and personality, hardiness and stress, hardiness and health, hardiness and illness etc. But no study has been done on hardiness in relation to alcoholism. Thus, we have taken hardiness as a variable in relation to alcohol use for the present study.

Hardiness as a Personality Construct

The term hardiness was introduced by Kobasa (1979) to refer to the personality style which keeps the person healthy even after prolonged exposure to stress. Hardy people are hypothesized to possess three general characteristics: commitment, control & challenge.

Commitment

Hardy people show deeper involvement in whatever they do and have a tendency to perceive these activities as worth doing. Persons strong in commitment have a strong sense of purpose and direction and do not easily give up under pressure. Commitment is reflected in the ability to feel activity involved with others and a belief in the truth, value and importance of one's self and one's experience (Huang & Wagnitd, 1995; Tartasky, 1993). Adverse situations are ultimately seen as meaningful and interesting (Maddi & Kobasa, 1984).

Control

They have a tendency to feel and act in an influential manner in the face of varied contingencies of life. They feel both capable and empowered to achieve desired outcomes (Kobasa, 1979). They act as they are influential in contingencies of life, events are perceived as a natural outgrowth to the individuals actions and not as unexpected experiences (Kobasa et al., 1982).

Challenge

Hardy people tend to perceive changes as a challenge, for them anticipation of changes are interesting incentives to growth rather than threat to security. Challenge reflects the belief that change is not a threat to personal security, but an opportunity for personal development and growth (Maddi & Kobasa, 1984). Hardiness reduces unhealthy effects of stress in two ways: (1) it improves health by acting as a buffer to stressful life events (Kobasa & Puccetti, 1983) and (2) it directly reduces the strain by decreasing the use of unsuccessful coping strategies (Kobasa et al., 1982).

22

Together, these characteristics mitigate the potential unhealthy effects of stress and prevent the organismic strain that often leads to illness. In contrast, non hardy or less hardy individuals easily succumb to ill effects of health as they find their environment boring, meaningless and threatening .They have a belief that life is best without change and allow external forces to impinge upon them and not try to transform the events by taking decisive   actions. Kobasa (1979) demonstrated the link between hardiness and health in a study of high stressed executives. She identified two groups of individuals, one who experienced high level of stress and severe illness, and another who had experienced high level of stress but little illness. Kobasa found that although, both the groups have experienced high levels of stress, low illness group was more hardy as compare to the high illness group. The high stress/low illness executives reported a greater sense of control, commitment and challenge than the high stress and high illness individuals did.

Thus hardiness (commitment, control & challenge) may play an important role in degree of alcohol use. If an individual is having strong commitment, control and accept the challenges positively he may not indulge in substance abuse/alcohol misuse and may help in constraining it to social drinking.

SELF-ESTEEM

Self Esteem refers to an individual's sense of his or her value or worth, or the extent to which a person values, approves of, appreciates, prizes or likes him or herself. The most broad and frequently cited definition of self esteem is by Rosenberg (1965), who described it as a favorable or unfavorable attitude towards the self. Self esteem is generally considered the evaluative component of the self concept, a broader representation of the self that includes cognitive and behavioral aspects as well as evaluative or affective ones. While the construct is most often used to refer to a global sense of self worth, narrower concepts such as self confidence or body esteem are used to imply a sense of self esteem in more specific domains. It is also widely assumed that self esteem functions as a trait, that is, it is stable across time within individuals (Blascovich & Tomaka, 1991).

Characteristics of High and Low Self-esteem

Rosenberg's conceptualization of self-esteem is heavily slanted toward the positive. He saw the high self-esteem person as likely to seek personal growth, development and improvement by pushing themselves to the limits to exercise their capabilities. He characterised the individual with high self-esteem as not having feelings of superiority, in the sense of arrogance, conceit, contempt for others, overwhelming pride. Rather he saw it as having self-respect, considering oneself a person of work, appreciating one's own merits, yet recognizing personal faults. The person with high self-esteem doesn't consider himself better than others, but neither does he consider himself inferior to others.

Rosenberg found that a deficient sense of the self has a profound impact on psychological functioning and mental health as well as on interpersonal behavior. He found that low self-esteem people are more likely to feel awkward, shy, conspicuous, and unable to express themselves with confidence. The low self-esteem person is always worried about making a mistake, being embarrassed or exposing themselves to ridicule. For low self-esteem people the self is a tender and delicate object, sensitive to the slightest touch. They have a strong incentive to avoid people or circumstances that reflect negatively on their feelings of self-worth. They are hypersensitive and hyper alert to signs of rejection, inadequacy or rebuff. They tend to adopt a characteristic strategy for dealing with life that is protective and defensive.

They are more depressed and unhappy; they have greater levels of anxiety; they show greater impulse to aggression, irritability, and resentment, and suffer from a lack of satisfaction with life in general. They have greater vulnerability to criticism, less self-concept stability, less faith in humanity and greater social anxiety. Virtually every feature of the low self-esteem personality undercuts spontaneity and creativity.

They tend to look for evidence that they are inadequate whereas high self-esteem people are motivated to discover evidence confirming their strengths. For low self-esteem individuals accepting positive feedback is a more subtle kind of risk than accepting negative feedback. Where successful performers attribute their successful outcomes to internal characteristics, low self-esteem individuals contribute success to external influences. Thus, their general approach to life is avoiding risk and embarrassment. As a result, they are never able to discover what they can do or be. This results in individual pain and loss of human potential.

Low self esteem is the universal common denominator among literally all people suffering from addictions to any and all mind altering substances such as alcohol. Alcohol use is simply a ramification and bad habit. People drink to suppress and escape their low self esteem. It's a bad habit we adopt for the sensation of "escape", as a sedative to relieve us of our anxieties, our stress, our fears in life, our fears of others, and our feelings of being inferior to others, all ramifications of our low self esteem. Alcohol is but a symptom of our real disease of low self esteem.

Relationship between Alcohol Abuse and Self-esteem

Low self esteem ultimately worsens and becomes further aggravated and compounded as life's inner and outer conflicts and problems continue, in our interpersonal relationships and in our love lives, and in every other area of our lives on the job and off the job, in the home and outside the home. Low self esteem plagues and corrupts our professional lives and our private lives.

Keegan (1987) investigated low self-esteem either causes or contributes to neurosis, anxiety, defensiveness, and ultimately alcohol and drug abuse.

Skager (1988) Found, self-esteem is indeed involved in addictive substance use. The use of drugs is often used to compensate for low self-esteem and feelings of a lack of control over one's life. Those with a strong sense of self do not have to be sustained at the expense of others. They do not need to control or humiliate other people or resort to substance abuse to compensate for low self esteem.

Effects of Alcoholism on Self-esteem

Alcohol is a commonly used substance among people all over the world. With its intoxicating effects and potential for abuse, a significant amount of research has been devoted to understanding the effects alcohol has on the human body, understanding what type of people consume alcohol, and understanding who is at risk for developing alcohol addiction. Although there is a significant amount of research devoted to alcohol, there are still many questions yet to be investigated. For instance, research has been conducted on how self-esteem influences alcohol consumption, but research on the reverse association of how alcohol consumption influence self-esteem has been neglected. There is a significant amount of research on the relationship between self-esteem and alcohol, focusing on how self-esteem influences who is likely to consume alcohol. Research shows that low self-esteem is negatively correlated with alcohol consumption.

Consuming alcohol and level of self-esteem have both been shown to be related to a person's mood. In an experiment by

McCollam, Burish, Maisto, & Sobell (1980), participants who consumed alcohol reported significantly higher levels of positive affect, such as elation, than sober participants. In addition, sober participants reported being more depressed than intoxicated participants. Similarly, Diener & Emmons (1985), found that self-esteem is also positively correlated with positive affect; participants with higher self-esteem reported being happier and joyful than participants with low self-esteem. These results show that both alcohol intoxication and high self-esteem have the same relationship with mood.

Different people have different levels of self esteem. Some people think they are wonderful while others think they are worthless. People with drugs or alcohol problems often have low self esteem. They judge themselves negatively- not just for their addiction but also for other parts of their behavior or their personality. Such negativity about themselves would influence their capability in dealing with life or coping with life events. So they might then turn to alcohol to deal with those feelings, if only temporarily. From there they may come to rely or depend on them.

Then of course the habitual use of substance/alcohol may further damage self esteem and reinforce those negative beliefs, which may lead to alcohol dependence/drug dependence. Thus self esteem may play a key role in maintaining the vicious circle around use of different levels of alcohol use.

LEARNED HELPLESSNESS

In both animals and humans, alcohol consumption and learned helplessness are clearly related but alcohol use typically increases following the trauma. It was found in a study with rats that there was very modest increase in alcohol consumption on days when shocks were administered but dramatic increases in alcohol on subsequent days (Volpicelli, Ulm, & Hopson, 1990). It is noted that even among social drinkers, alcohol consumption increases following the traumatic event but not during.

The model of learned helplessness given by Seligman(1973) describes states of helplessness that exist in humans who have experienced numerous failures (either real or perceived).The individual abandons any further attempts toward success. Seligman theorized that learned helplessness predisposes individuals to depression by imposing a feeling of lack of control over their life situations (McKinney & Moran, 1982). It has been empirically proven that negative expectations about the effectiveness of one's own efforts in bringing about the control over one's own environment leads to passivity and diminished initiation of responses (Abrahmson, Seligman & Teasdale, 1978). The term learned helplessness describes an organism's reaction when it is faced with important events that cannot be altered by its voluntary responses. Learned helplessness is both a behavioral state and a personality trait of one who believes that control has been lost over the reinforces in the environment. These negative expectations lead to helplessness, passivity and an inability to assert oneself.

Learned helplessness is a psychological condition in which a human or animal has learned to believe that they are helpless. They feel that they have no control over their situation and that whatever they do is futile. As a result, they will stay passive when the situation is unpleasant, harmful or damaging. Learned helplessness undermines motivation and retards the ability to perceive success (Seligman, 1975). Martin Seligman developed the theory of depression in the mid 1960's. The theory has two main points, people become depressed when they think that they no longer have control over the reinforcements (the rewards and punishments) in their lives and that they themselves are responsible for this helpless state. Not all people become depressed as a result of being in a situation where they appear not to have control. Seligman discovered that a depressed person thought about the bad event in more pessimistic ways than a non-depressed person. He called this thinking, "explanatory style". People in a state of learned helplessness view problems as personal, pervasive, or permanent. That is, Personal - they may see themselves as the problem; that is, they have internalized the problem. Pervasive - they may see the problem as affecting all aspects of life. Permanent - they may see the problem as unchangeable.

It is a motivational problem where one might have failed in a task or two in the past which have made that individual believe that they are incapable to do anything in order to improve their performance in that task (Stipek & Freeman, 1988).

Relationship between Learned Helplessness and Alcoholism

It is a motivational problem where one might have failed in a task or two in the past which have made that individual believe that they are incapable to do anything in order to improve their performance in that task (Stipek & Freeman, 1988).Most humans have an intrinsic need to be competent and to explore behaviors. If they fail, their competence diminishes, and they feel no need to explore. This is when one becomes helpless (Shield, 1988). Symptoms of learned helplessness are few voluntary responses, only answers to direct inquiries; Negative thinking and difficulty learning how to act to effect the outcome; Passivity in all situations; Increase of all of the above over time; Depressed appetite, sexual interest, less socialization, lack of self care, no desire to put out any energy; Physiological changes such as weight loss or gain. The helplessness syndrome can result from stimulus deprivation due to isolation, or from a combination of these things. Individuals experiencing reactions to grief and loss may also exhibit symptoms of the helplessness syndrome (Seligman, 1975).

So, feelings of learned helplessness might influence the individual's use/abuse of alcohol in the face of stressful situations. In this condition the individual assumes that he cannot control the situations or environment and simply stops trying to make things better and starts taking substance/alcohol to control the situations. Further the learned helplessness may pre dispose him towards dependence rather than controlled drinking.

Alcohol is by far the most commonly abused drug among the adult population. The health care system is greatly affected by alcoholism. In India, 10% of adults entering private physician's clinics are alcoholics and 15-40% of adult admissions to general hospitals are for alcohol related problems. (W.H.A. Report, 2002). One fact comes to the forefront while analyzing the whole scenario that is what makes certain drinkers strictly remain social drinkers while others further deteriorate to drinking as a habit and become addicts/dependents.

Being a resident of Punjab and having worked in various de-addiction centers, I have confronted problems through various young patients tend to fall and their relapse rate is high directly influencing general and psychological well being of their respective families. The subject himself suffers from a range of allied problems ranging from accidental traumas to more specific diseases like mental disorders and liver diseases. In this study the researcher aims to understand/establish the proportionality between the alcohol intake with different characteristics of personality in terms of hardiness, conceptualization of acceptance and regard for one self in terms of self-esteem and the feelings of not having any effective control over life events in terms of learned helplessness.

The primary focus of the research is to aid counseling and de-addiction of the subjects as well as education of the affected families through a scientifically proven approach which would include hardiness, self-esteem, learned helplessness and their relation with different levels of alcohol use.

AIMS AND OBJECTIVES

1) To determine the relationship between hardiness and different levels of alcohol use.

2) To determine the relationship between self-esteem and different levels of alcohol use.

3) To determine the relationship between learned helplessness and different levels of alcohol use.

4) To determine relative contribution of hardiness, self esteem and learned helplessness on different levels of alcohol use.

THEORETICAL ORIENTATION

From the previous discussion there is a little doubt that alcoholism is related to certain personality type or characteristics but to what extent certain personality characteristics effect the alcohol use in adulthood is still to be understood. Studies have been done on drug abuse and personality but little work have been done on the hardiness, self-esteem and learned helplessness in relation to alcohol use. Since the present problem is related to the problem of alcoholism and its relation to different characteristics of personality, it is therefore necessary first to have conceptual clarification about the concept of alcoholism and have operational definitions of the same.

The term 'alcoholism' is a widely used term, but in medicine was replaced in by 'alcohol abuse' and 'alcohol dependence' in the 1980s DSM III. Similarly in 1979 an expert World Health Organisation committee disfavoured the use of 'alcoholism' as a diagnostic entity, preferring the category of "alcohol dependence syndrome". In the 19th and early 20th centuries, alcohol dependence was called dipsomania, before the term alcoholism replaced it.

Alcoholism is conceptualized as being at the extreme of the drinking continuum so that it emerges from normal drinking behaviour rather than being artificially separated from it. It is also views alcoholism as more is a syndrome and less as a discrete condition. Alcoholism is the intermittent or continual ingestion of alcohol, leading to dependence or harm (Jellineck's, 1966).

34

"Alcoholism is a primary, chronic disease with genetic, psychosocial, and environmental factors influencing its development and manifestations. The disease is often progressive and fatal. It is characterized by continuous or periodic: impaired control over drinking, preoccupation with the drug alcohol, use of alcohol despite adverse consequences, and distortions in thinking, most notably denial."

THEORIES OF ALCOHOLISM

The causes of alcoholism are unknown, but many theories have been formulated, usually based on the background and clinical experiences of the scientists.

1.   Psychoanalytic view point

Freud (1925) has mentioned the reactivation or repressed homosexual traits as the basic conflicts causing the extensive use of alcohol.

Knight (1937) emphasized early childhood development as leading to alcoholism. He sees the alcohol as alleviating disappointment and rage. It is used as a mean to carry out repressed impulses in order to secure masochistic debasement and as a symbolic gratification of the need for affection.

Menninger (1938) emphasized the self-destructive drives of the alcoholic and term alcoholism as chronic suicide.

Fenichel (1945) maintains that alcoholics are passive dependent and have a predominantly oral-narcissistic orientation.

Tiebout (1951) believes that the alcoholic has an unconscious wish to dominate his environment. He feels that a pervasive feeling of loneliness and isolation is one of the main characteristic of the alcoholic.

2.   Learning (Re-inforcement) Theory

This theory basically postulates that if an action leads in a relatively short time to a desired effect, the individual is induced to repeat the action to get the same or an even more desirable effect. Alcohol consumption reduces an individual's feelings of tension and unpleasantness and replaces these feelings with one of well-being and euphoria, which can be observed in people after one or more drinks. Alcohol is the ideal rein-forcer of drinking behaviour.

Re-inforcement theories are based on the premise that people begin drinking, drink abusively and remain alcoholic because alcohol serves some useful purpose i.e. the drinking behaviour is rewarded or re-inforced. The reward could be the induction of pleasurable psychological changes, the removal of discomfort or having other enjoyable experiences (Bandura, 1969., Roebuck & Kesseler, 1972).

Alterman, Gottheil & Crawford (1975) observed that the specific effects of alcohol on tension and mood appear to be related to the amount and time of drinking as well as the specific circumstances in which alcohol intake occurs.

3.   Final Common Pathway Theory

Mc cord & Mc cord (1962) revealed that the final common pathway of different characteristics and systems have come together to produce the addictive drinker. All aspects of an individual's life play a part here; his childhood traumas, familial structure, peer groups and social group, stated reversely, absence of these factors will probably prevent an individual from abusing alcohol.

4.   Power-Status Theory

Mark, Frances, Okum (1986) stated that the power-status approach to alcoholism states, negative emotions that result from outcomes of social relations are subject differential coping responses e.g. consuming alcohol.

5.   Personality Trait Theory

Many Researchers have attempted to define the causes of alcoholism in terms of an "Alcoholic personality". Although it is felt that all alcoholics do not have the same personality structure, it is postulated that in the pre-alcoholic stage a personality pattern could be recognized as a predisposition toward alcoholism.

Lisansky (1960) suggested that the alcoholic personality has 1. An intensely strong need for dependency 2. A weak and inadequate defence against this excessive need, leading to intense dependence – independence conflicts. 3. A low degree of tolerance for frustration or tension and 4. Unresolved love hate ambivalences.

Blane (1970) has presented some of the personality characteristics commonly seen in alcoholics. They include low frustration tolerance, sociability, feeling of inferiority combined with attitudes of superiority, fearfulness, and dependency.

6.   Deviant Behaviour Theory

Sutherland & Cressley (1960)., Becker (1963)., Lemart (1967) many researchers through their researches have tried to prove that alcohol abuse as a deviant behaviour.

7.   Cultural Theory

From the view point of drinking as a symptom, Horton (1959) noted that its nearly universal occurrence and its survival as a custom, suggests its high acceptability and utilitarian function in society.

Bales (1959) proposed three ways in which culture and social organisation can influence the rates of alcoholism 1. The degree to which the culture operates to bring about inner tensions or acute needs for adjustment in its members 2. The attitudes toward drinking the culture produces in its members and 3. The degree to which the culture provides suitable substitute means of satisfaction.

8.   Socio-culture Theories

Socio-cultural theories have for the most part been generated by observations of similarities and differences between cultural groups and subgroups. Cultural theories can be viewed from two perspectives: the level of culture being examined and the level of drinking.

On a supracultural level, Bacon (1974) believes that alcoholism occurs in any society combining a lack of indulgence of children with demanding attitudes toward achievement and a restrictive posture toward dependent behaviour in adults.

Culture specific and subcultural theories regard alcoholism as a result of downward social mobility (e.g. job, income) possibly beginning before the problem drinking. This can result from an inability of the individual to participate in opportunities of the community, which might generate frustrations and result in alcoholic patterns.

PHYSIOLOGY OF ALCOHOLISM

The major intoxicant of the beers, wines and spirits that we drink is a clear, colourless, somewhat volatile liquid, ethyl alcohol. Ethyl alcohol is one of the series of alcohols. Wines, beers and spirits have characteristic difference in colour, taste and smell but what is important for the student of alcoholism is that they all contain, in different proportions, the active substance ethyl alcohol. The various drinks and their approximate strength expressed as a percentage of pure alcohol by volume are listed in the following table.

Beverage	% alcohol by volume
Beer and ale	4-8
Table wine	11-14
Fortified wine (Sheery, portory)	18-23
Spirits (whisky, Rum, Brandy, Gin)	35-50

Alcohol is unusual in that it is both a drug and a food stuff. As a food, it is a rich source of energy, yielding 7 cal/gm of alcohol. It is therefore yields more energy than an equivalent amount of protein or carbohydrate and only slightly less energy than an equivalent amount of fat. Furthermore, since does not require to be digested, but it is taken up unchanged from the stomach to blood stream, it is a rapid source of energy. It is nevertheless a poor food since it lacks proteins, vitamins and other nutrients.

Indeed, if alcohol is taken in excess, it is a potent cause of malnutrition. Since it is rich source of calories, if a full diet is taken it disturbs the usual balance between carbohydrate, proteins and fats and this may have deleterious consequences. It discourages taking of a full diet.

EFFECTS OF ALCOHOL

Alcohol is a member of that group of depressant drugs which includes the volatile anaesthesia. It has many properties in common with these drugs and it is itself an anaesthetic and pain killer.

Alcohol produces its effect on the body and on behaviour in different ways. Some effect follows a direct toxic effect of alcohol or some of its breakdown products on the cells of the central nervous system and the cells of the liver. A further group of symptoms, collectively known as withdrawal symptoms, arise when the physically dependent alcoholic is deprived of alcohol.

Immediate Effects

The well-known immediate consequence of drinking alcohol is acute intoxication. Individuals vary greatly in their ability to tolerate alcohol. The speed of drinking, the total dose consumed and the various factors, which modify rates of absorption, are all therefore important determinants of the degree of intoxication.

At low dose levels, alcohol has a slight stimulating effect on the brain (Kalant, 1975) but this is soon overtaken by a depressant action which affects early areas of the brain responsible for the integration and control of complex thinking, feeling and behavior.

At higher dose levels, thinking become low and superficial and learning and retention of information become faulty. Less attention is paid to stimuli from without and within so that feelings e. g. of hunger or pain is ignored etc.

Approximate correlations between blood alcohol level and behavior level given below

Blood Alcohol	Behavior Level
30 mg/100ml	Mild feeling of well being.
50 mg/100ml	Slight unsteadiness, Nystagmus probable,

                    Obvious ataxia

100 mg/100ml   Nystagmus present

300 mg/100ml   Stuporose

500 mg/100ml   Coma and death

Long term effects of Alcohol

The development of tolerance and dependence are two important effects of the chronic administration of alcohol. The usual symptoms of withdrawal in the physically dependent alcohol are tremulousness, convulsions and delirium. Mentally the patient is confused. He is hallucinated. Alcohol has long term effects on many of the organs of the body, notably brain and the heart. The heart is also affected by alcohol. Alcohol is an important cause of anemia, which is associated with many different kinds of skin and eye conditions. The extent of the damage is related to the age of the drinker, to the length of the time he has been drinking and to the amount of his drinking. Treatment in hospital is desirable. Usually the response to treatment is satisfactory but occasionally deaths occur.

The psychological effects of alcohol are conductive to acts of aggression in some individuals. Fear and anxieties are reduced and the intoxicated person's perceptions of the world are changed. He seems himself and the people around him as different. He has tendency to perceive feelings and events with greater sensitivity and to misinterpret the intentions of others. For a person on the threshold of committing a crime, alcohol often provides the calmness, resolution and courage to diminish realistic fears. Alcohol also diminishes the drinker's fear of external punishment and chastisement from his own conscience. Thus, the intoxicated individual sheds many of his guilt feelings.

THEORIES OF PERSONALITY

Freud Psychoanalytic theory – it includes a theory of personality structure, with id as a store house of unconscious drives and impulses; the super ego as conscience; and the ego as executive force, or mediator, balancing the pressures of id and superego with the constraints of reality. Freud also described the stages of psychosexual development (oral, anal, phallic, latency, and genital) and proposed that puzzling events such as dreams and slips of tongue" reveal unconscious impulses and conflicts.

Inter-personal Theory- Man is a social being. His behavior grows out of his attempts to establish a meaningful relationship with others. Significant contributions to the inter-personal theory was made by Harry, Adolf & Eric (1928).

Sullivan described the basic principles of the inter-personal theory as

1) Iner-personal relationship and the personality development. He believed, like Freud, that development proceeds through various stages. But he described how in each stage there is involvement of different pattern of relationship. For instance, infancy brings interactions with parents and there is need for contact. In childhood, more interactions with adults by

43

participation in activities is required. In the stages of pre-adolescence and adolescence, there is gradual withdrawal of the child from parents; peer relationship becomes important. In late adolescence or early adulthood, intimate relationship with hetrosexual groups are established, resulting in marital setting.

2) Other aspect of the theory is anxiety which has relationship in the formation of the personality. Since the infant is completely dependent on 'significant others' such as mother or father, mother figure like aunt for meeting his physical or psychological needs, lack of any these needs will lead him/her to an insecure and anxious human being. In early childhood, if he/she perceives himself/herself being rejected he/she will have a negative self concept which will lead him/her to maladjustment.

3) Socialisation causes a lot of pressure on children. Appreciation and praise by others will enable the child to label him/her as "Good me" and criticism may lead to the label of "Bad me". Over a period an individual develops a self system by using defence mechanism to reduce anxiety of socialisation pressures.

4) The other important aspects of the inter-personal theory are social exchange, social role and inter-personal accommodation.

Behavioral Theory

Behavioral theory is based on the concept that all bahavior, adaptive or maladaptive, is a product of learning. The contributors to this theory are Watson (1928), Pavlov (1960) & Skinner(1972).The basic assumptions of this theory are:

1) Behavior is a response to stimuli from the environment and reinforcement is essential to get response. Positive reinforcement is a reward for selected behaviour. Every time a child draws a good picture, the mother pat on his or her back. In negative reinforcement one would like to avoid a response from a child. Human personality is a combination of stimulus - response habits. Neurotic symptoms viewed as learned habits or responses that are repeatedly reinforced. Maladaptive behaviour can be unlearned and replaced by adaptive behaviour if the person receives appropriate stimulus to eliminate the maladaptive learning.

Personality traits are five broad factors or dimensions of personality discovered through empirical research (Goldberg, 1993). These factors are often called **Openness, Conscientiousness, Extraversion, Agreeable, and Neuroticism;** in this form, they are also referred to as the Five Factor Model (FFM) are discussed below.

FIVE FACTOR MODEL OF PERSONALITY

Openness to Experience

Openness to Experience describes a dimension of personality that distinguishes imaginative, creative people from down-to-earth, conventional people. Open people are intellectually curious, appreciative of art, and sensitive to beauty. They tend to be, compared

45

to closed people, more aware of their feelings. They therefore tend to hold unconventional and individualistic beliefs, although their actions may be conforming. People with low scores on openness to experience tend to have narrow, common interests. They prefer the plain, straightforward, and obvious over the complex, ambiguous, and subtle. They may regard the arts and sciences with suspicion, regarding these endeavors as of no practical use. Closed people prefer familiarity over novelty; they are conservative and resistant to change.

Conscientiousness

Conscientiousness concerns the way in which we control, regulate, and direct our impulses. Impulses are not inherently bad; occasionally time constraints require a snap decision, and acting on our first impulse can be an effective response. Also, in times of play rather than work, acting spontaneously and impulsively can be fun. Impulsive individuals can be seen by others as colorful, fun-to-be-with. Conscientiousness includes the factor known as Need for Achievement (NAch).

The benefits of high conscientiousness are obvious. Conscientious individuals avoid trouble and achieve high levels of success through purposeful planning and persistence. They are also positively regarded by others as intelligent and reliable. On the negative side, they can be compulsive perfectionists and workalcoholics.

Extraversion

Extraversion (also "extroversion") is marked by pronounced engagement with the external world. Extraverts enjoy being with people, are full of energy, and often experience positive emotions. They tend to be enthusiastic, action-oriented individuals who are likely to say "Yes!" or "Let's go!" to opportunities for excitement. In groups they like to talk, assert themselves, and draw attention to themselves.

Introverts lack the exuberance, energy, and activity levels of extraverts. They tend to be quiet, low-key, deliberate, and less dependent on the social world. Their lack of social involvement should not be interpreted as shyness or depression; the introvert simply needs less stimulation than an extravert and more time alone to re-charge his batteries.

A simple explanation is that an extrovert gains energy by associating with others and loses energy when alone for any period of time. An introvert is the opposite, as they gain energy from doing individual activities such as watching movies or reading and lose energy, sometimes to the point of exhaustion, from social activities.

Agreeableness

Agreeableness reflects individual differences in concern with cooperation and social harmony. Agreeable individuals have an optimistic view of human nature, and value getting along with others; they are therefore considerate, friendly, generous, helpful, and willing to compromise with others. Disagreeable individuals place self-interest above getting along with others. They are generally unconcerned with others' well-being, and are less likely to extend themselves for other people. Agreeableness is obviously advantageous for attaining and maintaining popularity, as Agreeable people are better liked than disagreeable people. On the other hand, agreeableness is detrimental in situations that require tough or absolute objective decisions..

Neuroticism

Neuroticism, also known inversely as Emotional Stability, refers to the tendency to experience negative emotions. Those who score high on Neuroticism may experience primarily one specific negative feeling such as anxiety, anger, or depression, but are likely to experience several of these emotions. People high in Neuroticism are emotionally reactive. They respond emotionally to events that would not affect most people, and their reactions tend to be more intense than normal. They are more likely to interpret ordinary situations as threatening, and minor frustrations as hopelessly difficult. Their negative emotional reactions tend to persist for unusually long periods of time, which means they are often in a bad mood. These problems in emotional regulation can diminish a neurotic's ability to think clearly, make decisions, and cope effectively with stress.

THE RELATIONSHIP BETWEEN PERSONALITY AND ALCOHOLISM

There are a numbers of ways that personality and alcoholism can be related; some of these are substantively important.

It is always important to remember that correlation between personality variables and alcoholism can be obtained because of unrecognized confounds at the measurement on design level, some personality scales contain items that directly reference substance use. As a case in point, disinhibition subscale of the sensation-seeking scale-version V (Zuckerman, & Eysenck,1977) is a frequently employed self-report measure of sensation seeking and impulsivity containing two items that directly asses substance use.(I often like to get high). I feel best after taking a couple of drinks. Failure to address this confounding of item content inflates the magnitude of the correlation between disinhibition and alcohol consumption.(Darkes, Greenbaum, & Goldman,1998).

Causal versus Non-causal Relationship

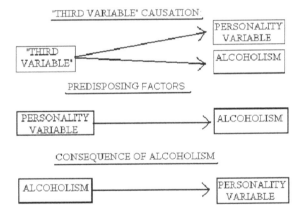

Figure: 1 Three basic models of the relationship between personality variables and alcoholism: (1) spurious ("third variable") relation. (2) Etiological (predisposing variable) relation, and (3) consequential relation.

Also, it is possible that personality and alcoholism can be spuriously related because of "third variable" causation. For example, throughout the adult years, alcoholism is more prevalent among males than among females. However many personality variables are related to gender (Costa & Mc Crae, 1992).

Direction of Influence- Besides from spurious relations, research on personality and alcoholism has suggested several models relating personality to alcohol use and abuse.

First, there are those models that posit personality as a predisposing factor. In these models, personality traits are thought to lead to alcoholism for any of a number of reasons. Personality traits could provide the primary motivational basis for alcohol consumption (eg. Negative affects regulation sensation seeking).Alternatively, personality traits could affect the likelihood that an individual who is already drinking is likely to continue drinking despite the fact that alcohol is interfering with his or her life.(eg. deficits in inhibitory control). Yet a third possibility is that personality traits contribute to the development of specific alcohol related consequences (eg. alcohol related aggression) in someone who has consumed alcohol (eg. in individuals high in trait aggressiveness).

The Relation of Personality with other Causal Variables

It is found that personality variables are viewed in the context of mediating and moderating relationship (Miller, 1995).

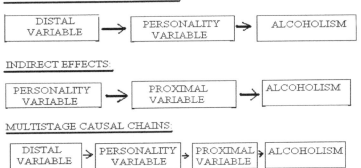

MEDIATING DISTAL VARIABLES:

| DISTAL VARIABLE | → | PERSONALITY VARIABLE | → | ALCOHOLISM |

INDIRECT EFFECTS:

| PERSONALITY VARIABLE | → | PROXIMAL VARIABLE | → | ALCOHOLISM |

MULTISTAGE CAUSAL CHAINS:

| DISTAL VARIABLE | → | PERSONALITY VARIABLE | → | PROXIMAL VARIABLE | → | ALCOHOLISM |

Figure: 2 Three basic models in which personality plays mediating & moderating roles.

First, personality variables have been posited to mediate the effects of more distal variables, such as family history on outcome (Cloninger, 1987., Sher et al, 2000).

Second, personality variables have been viewed as having only indirect effects on disorders; that is their primary effects are mediated by other variables more proximal to outcome. To illustrate the notion of an indirect effect, it has been posited that individuals who are high on trait related to negative affectivity are more likely to experience subjective distress and consequently turn to alcohol for 'self-medication' purposes (Sher et al, 2000).

Sher et al suggested that the effect of family history on offspring alcoholism could be mediated by such a multistage chain where family history (a distal variable) is related to behavioral under control (a personality variable) which in turn is related to alcohol outcome

51

expectancies (a proximal variable) which in turn is related to alcohol involvement.

In addition to mediating type relationship, there is ample evidence to suggest that personality can play a moderating role in alcohol use and alcoholism, interacting with various risk factors to exacerbate the likelihood of consumption or disorder; that is, ones relative standing on a personality dimension can determine the strength of relation between a predictor variable and an alcohol related outcome. For example the trait of dispositional self awareness (a personality variable) has been shown to interact with life events (a predictor variable) in determining the likelihood of relapse (Hull & Young, 2005). Similarly self awareness has been shown to interact with family history of alcoholism in predicting offspring alcohol problems (Rogsch, Chassin & Sher, 1990) and appears to moderate the relationship between alcohol outcome expectancies and alcohol use (Bartholaw, & Sher , 2000).

HARDINESS

Hardiness as a Personality Construct

The term hardiness was introduced by Kobasa (1979) to refer to the personality style which keeps the person healthy even after prolonged exposure to stress. Hardy people are hypothesized to possess three general characteristics: commitment, control & challenge.

Commitment

Hardy people show deeper involvement in whatever they do and have a tendency to perceive these activities as worth doing. Persons strong in commitment have a strong sense of purpose and direction and do not easily give up under pressure. Commitment is reflected in the ability to feel activity involved with others and a belief in the truth, value and importance of one's self and one's experience (Huang & Wagnitd, 1995; Tartasky, 1993). Adverse situations are ultimately seen as meaningful and interesting (Maddi & Kobasa, 1984).

Control

They have a tendency to feel and act in an influential manner in the face of varied contingencies of life. They feel both capable and empowered to achieve desired outcomes (Kobasa, 1979). They act as they are influential in contingencies of life, events are perceived as a natural outgrowth to the individuals actions and not as unexpected experiences (Kobasa et al.,1982).

Hardiness Concept Map, Figure: 3

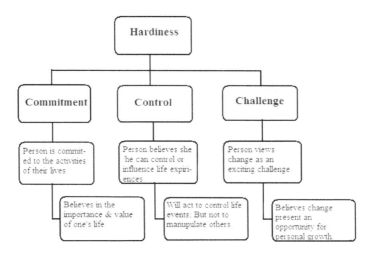

Challenge

Hardy people tend to perceive changes as a challenge, for them anticipation of changes are interesting incentives to growth rather than threat to security. Challenge reflects the belief that change is not a threat to personal security, but an opportunity for personal development and growth (Maddi & Kobasa, 1984). Hardiness reduces unhealthy effects of stress in two ways: (1) it improves health by acting as a buffer to stressful life events (Kobasa & Puccetti, 1983) and (2) it directly reduces the strain by decreasing the use of unsuccessful coping strategies (Kobasa et al., 1982).

SELF-ESTEEM

Self Esteem refers to an individual's sense of his or her value or worth, or the extent to which a person values, approves of, appreciates, prizes or likes him or herself. The most broad and frequently cited definition of self esteem is by Rosenberg (1965), who described it as a favorable or unfavorable attitude towards the self. Self esteem is generally considered the evaluative component of the self concept, a broader representation of the self that includes cognitive and behavioral aspects as well as evaluative or affective ones. While the construct is most often used to refer to a global sense of self worth, narrower concepts such as self confidence or body esteem are used to imply a sense of self esteem in more specific domains. It is also widely assumed that self esteem functions as a trait, that is, it is stable across time within individuals (Blascovich & Tomaka, 1991).

Cohen (1983) defined self-esteem as the degree of correspondence between an individual's ideal and actual concept of himself.

Coopersmith (1959) suggested four types of self-esteem namely: what a person purports to have, what he really has, what he displays, and what others believe he has. Self-esteem according to Coopersmith (1967) refers to individual's personal judgement of his own worth.

Gelfand (1962) defined self-esteem as "a person's characteristics evaluation of himself and what he thinks of himself as an individual".

Elder (1968) defined self-esteem as a "feeling of personal worth-influenced by performance, abilities, appearance and judgement of significant others".

Reflected appraisal is the impact that the evaluation of some one else, especially an important person such as a parent has.

Social comparison is the process of evaluating options, abilities, and personal traits by comparing them with the opinions, abilities and personal traits of other people.

Attributions is the process of inferring that one possesses certain traits by looking at the causes of one's behaviour, and where appropriate, seeing that they reflect personal characteristics.

Identification is the process of admiring or envying another person and trying to be as much like that person as possible.

Gergen (1971) proposed that self-esteem is the best thought of as a set of attitudes about the self which produces a different overall self evaluation depending upon the circumstances; it is not a global self evaluation.

Morrison, Thomas, & Weaver (1973) defined self-esteem as a "personality variable expected to influence a person's evaluation of his work".

Attempts have been made to relate personality factors to alcohol dependence. Potential alcoholics tend to be emotionally immature, expect a great deal of the world, require an inordinate amount of praise and appreciation, react to failure with marked feelings of hurt and inferiority, have a low frustration tolerance, and feel inadequate and unsure of their abilities to fulfill expected male or female roles. Certainly, many people with similar personality characteristics do not become alcoholics, and others with dissimilar ones do. One characteristic that appears common to the backgrounds of most problem drinkers is personal maladjustment, yet most maladjusted people do not become alcoholics. Although the significance of alcoholic personality factors remains unclear, researchers have shown that the personality of alcoholics significantly influences treatment outcome. Hence, an understanding of the personality characteristics associated with alcohol dependence may be useful for treatment.

THEORIES OF SELF-ESTEEM

Self-actualization Theory

Maslow(1970) mentioned in his theory the esteem needs (hierarchy of needs) beyond the details of air, water, food, and sex, he laid out five broader layers: the physiological needs, the needs for safety and security, the needs for love and belonging, the needs for esteem, and the need to actualize the self, in that order.

The esteem needs. Maslow noted two versions of esteem needs, a lower one and a higher one. The lower one is the need for the respect of others, the need for status, fame, glory, recognition, attention, reputation, appreciation, dignity, even dominance.

Figure: 4 Self-actualization theory

Being Needs

Self-actualization

Esteem Needs

Belonging Needs

Safety Needs

Physiological Needs

Deficit Needs

The higher form involves the need for self-respect, including such feelings as confidence, competence, achievement, mastery, independence, and freedom. Note that this is the "higher" form because, unlike the respect of others, once you have self-respect, it's a lot harder to lose!

1. **The physiological needs**. These include the needs we have for oxygen, water, protein, salt, sugar, calcium, and other minerals and vitamins. They also include the need to maintain a pH balance (getting too acidic or base will kill you) and temperature (98.6 or near to it). Also, there's the needs to be active, to rest, to sleep, to get rid of wastes (CO_2, sweat, urine, and feces), to avoid pain, and to have sex. Quite a collection!

Maslow believed, and research supports him, that these are in fact individual needs, and that a lack of, say, vitamin C, will lead to a very specific hunger for things which have in the past provided that vitamin C - e.g. orange juice. I guess the cravings that some pregnant women have, and the way in which babies eat the most foul tasting baby food, support the idea anecdotally.

2. **The safety and security needs**. When the physiological needs are largely taken care of, this second layer of needs comes into play. You will become increasingly interested in finding safe circumstances, stability, protection. You might develop a need for structure, for order, some limits.

Looking at it negatively, you become concerned, not with needs like hunger and thirst, but with your fears and anxieties. In the ordinary American adult, this set of needs manifest themselves in the form of our urges to have a home in a safe neighborhood, a little job security and a nest egg, a good retirement plan and a bit of insurance, and so on.

3. **The love and belonging needs**. When physiological needs and safety needs are, by and large, taken care of, a third layer starts to show up. You begin to feel the need for friends, a sweetheart, children, affectionate relationships in general, even a sense of community. Looked at negatively, you become increasing susceptible to loneliness and social anxieties.

In our day-to-day life, we exhibit these needs in our desires to marry, have a family, be a part of a community, a member of a church, a brother in the fraternity, a part of a gang or a bowling club. It is also a part of what we look for in a career.

4. **The esteem needs**. Next, we begin to look for a little self-esteem. Maslow noted two versions of esteem needs, a lower one and a higher one. The lower one is the need for the respect of others, the need for status, fame, glory, recognition, attention, reputation, appreciation, dignity, even dominance. The higher form involves the need for self-respect, including such feelings as confidence, competence, achievement, mastery, independence, and freedom. Note that this is the "higher" form because, unlike the respect of others, once you have self-respect, it's a lot harder to lose!

The negative version of these needs is low self-esteem and inferiority complexes. Maslow felt that Adler was really onto something when he proposed that these were at the roots of many, if not most, of our psychological problems. In modern countries, most of us have what we need in regard to our physiological and safety needs. We, more often than not, have quite a bit of love and belonging, too.

Sociometer Theory of Self-Esteem

Sociometer Theory explains the need and function of human self-esteem by stating that the sociometer is an internal gauge that moderates human behaviour to ensure that exclusion from the social group is unlikely to occur (Leary & Downs, 1995). It is an evolutionary based psychological theory referring to the fact that in earlier civilisations exclusion from a social group could result in the death of an individual.

Sociometer theory was initially theorised by Leary & Downs (1995) who stated that self-esteem is a mechanism by which an individual can assess their behaviour and current standing in his or her social group. Leary & Downs (1995) suggested that the sociometer, which they describe as being like a fuel gauge in a motor vehicle, is an internal system for monitoring a person's environment for cues that the person is being excluded or avoided.

According to Leary & Downs (1995), when the internal sociometer notes that there is a potential for exclusion, a negative affect is felt in the person; for example if a behaviour leads to being ignored or ridiculed, the person undertaking the behaviour may feel bad or upset.

Kirkpatrick & Ellis (2003) expanded on Leary and Downs' (1995) Sociometer Theory by suggesting that self-esteem has separate functions and domains across the human psyche, in order to monitor various types of social interactions and accordingly it is possible for there to be more than one internal sociometer. Kirkpatrick & Ellis (2003) suggested that the sociometer's function was not only to ensure that an individual was not excluded from their social group but also to rate the strength of the social group compared to other groups.

There is not a conclusive answer as to the theoretical basis of self-esteem. Empirical research in relation to Sociometer Theory has been undertaken by Anthony, Wood & Holmes (2007); Denissen, Penkie, Schmitt & van Aken (2008).

Anthony, Wood & Holmes (2007) tested Sociometer Theory's ability to explain and guide social behaviour. The researchers found that people with low levels of self-esteem were likely to express low levels of confidence in relation to being accepted by a new social group. Conversely and in accordance with the principles of Sociometer Theory, people with high levels of self-esteem did not report a fear of being rejected by the group (Anthony, Wood & Holmes, 2007).

Denissen, Penke, Schmitt & van Aken's (2008) research into close social relationships and self-esteem also supported the principles of Sociometer Theory. Denissen, Penke, Schmitt & van Aken (2008) found that day to day self-esteem is affected by the quality of interactions with family members and close friends. Sociometer Theory states that self-esteem's function is to monitor the environment for clues that behaviours are likely to result in exclusion from the social group.

The Sociometer Theory of self-esteem states that the purpose of self-esteem in human beings is to act as a behaviour monitor ensuring that the likelihood of exclusion from the social group is low. It has not been proved conclusively that the internal fuel gauge of the sociometer is responsible for individual feelings of self-esteem and self worth.

Terror Management Theory

Terror Management Theory states that the function of self-esteem is to reduce the anxiety of death by relating to and acting in ways that support a culturally based world view.

62

Greenberg, Pyszczynski & Solomon (1986) identified two components of self esteem relating to cultural beliefs and threat defences. Similar to the Sociometer Theory, Terror Management Theory is an evolutionary based psychological theory of human self-esteem.

According to Greenberg, Pyszczynski & Solomon (1986), cultural beliefs, symbols and values are important to self-esteem as they provide individuals with a sense of permanence and reality and provide an opportunity for immortality. Social situations which provide an opportunity for the cultural world view of an individual to be questioned can be a source of anxiety and a threat to self-esteem (Greenberg, Pyszczynski & Solomon, 1986).

Such threatening situations may only exist at a symbolic level however they can provide a negative affect to the self-esteem of the threatened individual (Greenberg, Pyszcynski & Solomon, 1986). Greenberg, Pyszczynski & Solomon (1986) also noted that threats were not limited to public events and that private awareness of failures could lead to negative affects in self-esteem.

Self-worth begins to develop in childhood and initially the sense of self-worth comes when a child meets the behaviour requirements set down by its parents. As self-consciousness develops, the child learns that feeling valued leads to pleasant outcomes and the avoidance of unpleasant or negative outcomes (Greenberg, Pyszczynski & Solomon, 1986).

Terror Management Theory suggests that from these early interactions develops the individual's sense of self-esteem which is used to decrease anxiety of mortality as an individual feels that provided they are acting in accordance with the cultural standards of their social group, the individual is of worth (Greenberg, Solomon, Pyszczynski, Rosenblatt, Burling, Lyon, Simon & Pinel, 1992).

Greenberg, et al (1992) experimentally tested the concepts of Terror Management Theory by undertaking three experiments to test the hypothesis that increasing self-esteem leads to a reduction in anxiety. The research found that increased self-esteem did reduce self-report anxiety and physiological arousal in relation to threats.

The results of Harmon-Jones, Simon, Greenberg, Pyszczynski, Solomon and McGregor's (1997) study of the concept of mortality salience supported the Terror Management Theory principle that high self esteem reduces anxiety caused by fear of death.

Terror Management Theory is an evolutionary based psychological theory of self-esteem explaining that the purpose of self-esteem is to assist individual human beings negate the fear of mortality through relating to and acting in ways which promote a cultural world view.

Social Identity Theory

Social Identity Theory was developed by Tajfel and Turner in 1979. The theory was originally developed to understand the psychological basis of intergroup discrimination. Tajfel, Flament,

Billig, & Bundy (1971) attempted to identify the minimal conditions that would lead members of one group to discriminate in favor of the ingroup to which they belonged and against another outgroup.

In the Social Identity Theory, a person has not one, "personal self", but rather several selves that correspond to widening circles of group membership. Different social contexts may trigger an individual to think, feel and act on basis of his personal, family or national "level of self" (Turner, Hogg, Oakes, Reicher, & Wetherell, 1987). Apart from the "level of self", an individual has multiple "social identities". Social identity is the individual's self-concept derived from perceived membership of social groups (Hogg & Terry, 2002). In other words, it is an individual-based perception of what defines the "us" associated with any internalized group membership. This can be distinguished from the notion of personal identity which refers to self-knowledge that derives from the individual's unique attributes.

Social Identity Theory asserts that group membership creates ingroup/ self-categorization and enhancement in ways that favor the in-group at the expense of the out-group. The examples (minimal group studies) of Turner and Tajfel (1986) showed that the mere act of individuals categorizing themselves as group members was sufficient to lead them to display ingroup favoritism. After being categorized of a group membership, individuals seek to achieve positive self-esteem by positively differentiating their ingroup from a comparison outgroup on some valued dimension. This quest for positive distinctiveness means that people's sense of who they are is defined in terms of 'we' rather than 'I'.

Tajfel & Turner (1979) identify three variables whose contribution to the emergence of ingroup favoritism is particularly important. A) the extent to which individuals identify with an ingroup to internalize that group membership as an aspect of their self-concept. B) the extent to which the prevailing context provides ground for comparison between groups. C) the perceived relevance of the comparison group, which itself will be shaped by the relative and absolute status of the ingroup. Individuals are likely to display favoritism when an ingroup is central to their self-definition and a given comparison is meaningful or the outcome is contestable.

Social Identity Theory has a considerable impact on social psychology. It is tested in a wide range of fields and settings and includes prejudice, stereotyping, negotiation and language use. The theory has also implications on the way people deal with social and organizational change.

In further research this example is referred to minimal group studies. Schoolboys were assigned to groups, which were intended as meaningless as possible. They were assigned randomly, excluding roles of interpersonal discrimination such as history of conflict, personal animosity or interdependence. The schoolboys assigned points to anonymous members of both their own group and the other group. Conclusions were that even the most minimal conditions were sufficient to encourage ingroup-favoring responses. Participants picked a reward pair that awarded more points to people who were identified as ingroup members. In other words, they displayed ingroup favoritism.

Self-evaluation or Self esteem Maintenance Theory

Self-evaluation maintenance theory refers to discrepancies between two people in a relationship. Two people in a relationship each aim to keep themselves feeling good psychologically throughout a comparison process to the other person.

Self-evaluation is defined as the way a person views him/herself. It is the continuous process of determining personal growth and progress, which can be raised or lowered by the behavior of a close other a person that is psychologically close. People are more threatened by friends than strangers.

RELATIONSHIP OF SELF ESTEEM TO HEALTH

Much of the research about the relationship between self-esteem and health appears to have been done in terms of the influence of self-esteem on health-related behaviors. Self-esteem has been related to such health practices as (Rivas, Torres, Fernandez & Fernandez, 1995) found that young adults with high self-esteem and high levels of knowledge about AIDS employed safer practices for non-conventional sexual practices than those with lower self-esteem, but were riskier than those with lower self-esteem for more conventional sexual practices.

Abood & Conway (1992) found a relationship between self-esteem and health values, and between self-esteem and general wellness behavior. The relationship between self-esteem and general wellness behavior remained significant even when health values were controlled for.

The well-established relationship between self-esteem and psychological well-being (e.g., depression, social anxiety, loneliness, alienation; Blascovich & Tomaka, (1991) may be an important factor in understanding the self-esteem/health relationship.

RELATIONSHIP BETWEEN ALCOHOL ABUSE AND SELF ESTEEM

Low self esteem is the universal common denominator among literally all people suffering from addictions to any and all mind altering substances such as alcohol. The problem and disease is entirely emotional, psychological, and sociological, as opposed to physiological. Low self esteem is the true problem and true disease.

Alcohol use is simply a ramification and bad habit. People drink to suppress and escape their low self esteem. It's a bad habit we adopt for the sensation of "escape", as a sedative to relieve us of our anxieties, our stress, our fears in life, our fears of others, and our feelings of being inferior to others, all ramifications of our low self esteem. Alcohol is but a symptom of our real disease of low self esteem.

Low self esteem is an intelligent awareness we have with regard to how others perceive us, an awareness that others think of us as

68

inferior and that others don't accept us. Individuals with defensive or low self-esteem typically focus on trying to prove themselves or impress others. They tend to use others for their own gain. Some act with arrogance and contempt towards others. They generally lack confidence in themselves, often have doubts about their worth and acceptability, and hence are reluctant to take risks or expose themselves to failure. They frequently blame others for their shortcomings rather than take responsibility for their actions.

Low self esteem ultimately worsens and becomes further aggravated and compounded as life's inner and outer conflicts and problems continue, in our interpersonal relationships and in our love lives, and in every other area of our lives on the job and off the job, in the home and outside the home. Low self esteem plagues and corrupts our professional lives and our private lives.

Keegan, (1987) investigated low self-esteem either causes or contributes to neurosis, anxiety, defensiveness, and ultimately alcohol and drug abuse.

Skager, (1988) Found, self-esteem is indeed involved in addictive substance use. The use of drugs is often used to compensate for low self-esteem and feelings of a lack of control over one's life. Those with a strong sense of self do not have to be sustained at the expense of others. They do not need to control or humiliate other people or resort to substance abuse to compensate for low self esteem.

EFFECTS OF ALCOHOLISM ON SELF ESTEEM

Alcohol is a commonly used substance among people all over the world. With its intoxicating effects and potential for abuse, a significant amount of research has been devoted to understanding the effects alcohol has on the human body, understanding what type of people consume alcohol, and understanding who is at risk for developing alcohol addiction. Although there is a significant amount of research devoted to alcohol, there are still many questions yet to be investigated. For instance, research has been conducted on how self-esteem influences alcohol consumption, but research on the reverse association of how alcohol consumption influence self-esteem has been neglected. There is a significant amount of research on the relationship between self-esteem and alcohol, focusing on how self-esteem influences who is likely to consume alcohol. Research shows that low self-esteem is negatively correlated with alcohol consumption.

Consuming alcohol and level of self-esteem have both been shown to be related to a person's mood. In an experiment by McCollam, Burish, Maisto, & Sobell (1980), participants who consumed alcohol reported significantly higher levels of positive affect, such as elation, than sober participants. In addition, sober participants reported being more depressed than intoxicated participants.

Different people have different levels of self esteem. Some people think they are wonderful while others think they are worthless. People with drugs or alcohol problems often have low self esteem. They judge themselves negatively- not just for their addiction but also for other parts of their behavior or their personality. Such negativity about themselves would influence their capability in dealing with life or coping with life events. So they might then turn to alcohol to deal with those feelings, if only temporarily. From there they may come to rely or depend on them.

Then of course the habitual use of substance / alcohol may further damage self esteem and reinforce those negative beliefs, which may lead to alcohol dependence/drug dependence. Thus self esteem may play a key role in maintaining the vicious circle around use of different levels of alcohol.

LEARNED HELPLESSNESS

Learned helplessness is a technical term which means a condition of a human being or an animal in which it has learned to behave helplessly, even when the opportunity is restored for it to help itself by avoiding an unpleasant or harmful circumstance to which it has been subjected.

A mental state in which people feel that they have no control over their failures and that failure is inevitable. Learned helplessness often occurs in children who are raised in harsh social environments where success is difficult to achieve. They suffer motivational losses and are very resistant to training.

Learned helplessness is a psychological state where people feel powerless to change their self or situation. This is primarily caused when people attribute negative things in life to internal, stable and global factors. Essentially, it means that the person feels as if change is not possible, since there is a pervasive and unchangeable personal problem.

The model of learned helplessness given by Seligman (1973) describes states of helplessness that exist in humans who have experienced numerous failures (either real or perceived).The individual abandons any further attempts toward success. Seligman theorized that learned helplessness predisposes individuals to depression by imposing a feeling of lack of control over their life situations (McKinney & Moran, 1982). It has been empirically proven that negative expectations about the effectiveness of one's own efforts in bringing about the control over one's own environment leads to passivity and diminished initiation of responses (Abrahmson, Seligman & Teasdale, 1978). The term learned helplessness describes an organism's reaction when it is faced with important events that cannot be altered by its voluntary responses. Learned helplessness is both a behavioral state and a personality trait of one who believes that control has been lost over the reinforcers in the environment. These negative expectations lead to helplessness, passivity and an inability to assert oneself.

Learned helplessness is a psychological condition in which a human or animal has learned to believe that they are helpless. They feel that they have no control over their situation and that whatever they do is futile. As a result, they will stay passive when the situation is unpleasant, harmful or damaging. Learned helplessness undermines motivation and retards the ability to perceive success (Seligman, 1975). Martin Seligman developed the theory of depression in the mid 1960's. The theory has two main points, people become depressed when they think that they no longer have control over the reinforcements (the rewards and punishments) in their lives and that they themselves are responsible for this helpless state. Not all people become depressed as a result of being in a situation where they appear not to have control. Seligman discovered that a depressed person thinks about the bad event in more pessimistic ways than a non-depressed person. He called this thinking, "explanatory style". People in a state of learned helplessness view problems as personal, pervasive, or permanent. That is, Personal - They may see themselves as the problem; that is, they have internalized the problem. Pervasive - They may see the problem as affecting all aspects of life. Permanent - They may see the problem as unchangeable.

It is a motivational problem where one might have failed in a task or two in the past which have made that individual believe that they are incapable to do anything in order to improve their performance in that task (Stipek & Freeman, 1988).

The Attributional Reformulation

Seligman's learned helplessness theory later reformulated. Abramson, Seligman & Teasdale (1978) redefined learned helplessness as "a consequence of perceptions of a noncontingency between one's responses desired outcomes". If the probably of reaching one's desired outcome is not increased by one's responses and desired outcomes is not increased by one's actions, then learned helplessness will result. The results are passivity, negative perceptions about future events, and generally negative perspective. In late 1970's, Seligman's theory of depression was reformulated within the framework of attribution theory (Gilbert, 1984). Briefly depression will occur if the individuals are aware of uncontrollable factors in their environment, view the situation as unchangeable, blames themselves for their helplessness-internal attribution (Seligman, 1992).

The original theory has been proved to be too simple for human behaviors, as not all people become depressed and react the same way after being in a situation they had no control over (Peterson & Park, 1998). Learned helplessness sometimes remains specific to one situation (Cole & Coyne, 1977) but sometimes generalizes across situations (Hiroto & Seligman, 1975).

Thereafter, Abraham, Seligman & Teasdale (1978) incorporated the elements of attribution theory to reformulate the theory of helplessness. The attribution theory by Weiner (1979, 1985, 1986) concerns the way people attribute causality to events. Whenever people encounter aversive events, people try to make causal explanation which includes the dimensions of globality, stability and internality (Weiner, 1986).

74

A global attribution occurs when the individual believes that the cause of negative events is consistent across different contexts, whereas a specific attribution occurs when the individual believes that the cause is unique to the particular situation. In addition, stable attribution occurs when the individual thinks that the cause is consistent across time, whereas unstable attribution occurs when the individual thinks that the cause is specific to one point in time. Furthermore, external attribution assigns causality to situation factors, while an internal attribution assigns causality to factors within the person (Abraham et. al., 1978).

Reformulated theory of learned helplessness proposes that explanatory style is the other determinant of causal explanation (Peterson & Seligman, 1984). Explanatory style refers to an individual's habitual way of assigning causes to negative events. Particular style, for example, a pessimistic explanatory style of causal attribution may lead to the loss of self-esteem, uncontrollability and then generality of helplessness (Peterson, Maier, & Seligman 1993).

RELATIONSHIP BETWEEN LEARNED HELPLESSNESS AND ALCOHOLISM

The effects of learned helplessness are lack of self confidence, poor problem solving, wandering attention and feeling hopeless. Other symptoms include; difficulty in learning behavior pattern in reaction to controllable adversities, reduced motivation in initiating coping responses and emotional reactions of sadness (Ramirez, Maldonado & Martos, 1992).

On the whole it can be concluded that feelings of learned helplessness might influence the individual's use of alcohol in the face of stressful situations. In this condition the individual assumes that he/she cannot control the situations or environment and simply stops trying to make things better and starts taking alcohol/substance to control the situations. Further the learned helplessness may pre dispose him/her towards dependence rather than controlled drinking.

REVIEW OF LITERATURE

A review of literature is essential in order to support the selection of variables and decide about the general framework of the study. Studies related to the present problem are reviewed in this chapter. Though the number of studies mentioned below may not be directly related to the present study, yet they are definitely essential for supporting the importance of the present study. The literature reviewed has been divided under the following subsections:

1) Alcoholism and Personality.

2) Alcoholism and Hardiness.

3) Alcoholism and Self-esteem.

4) Alcoholism and Learned Helplessness.

ALCOHOLISM AND PERSONALITY

The available researches suggest that personality and alcoholism are correlated. There are many studies which support the theory that personality affects the level of alcoholism among adult population.

In a meta-analysis the relationship between the Five-Factor Model of personality and alcohol involvement have shown and also identify moderators of the relationship. The meta-analysis included 20 studies and 7,886 participants. Possible moderators examined included: five-factor rating type (self vs. other); study time-frame (cross sectional vs. longitudinal); sample type (treatment vs. non-treatment); type of alcohol involvement measure used; gender of the participants; and age of the participants. The meta-analysis showed alcohol involvement was associated with low conscientiousness, low agreeableness, and high neuroticism (John, Einar, Thorsteinsson, Sally, Nicola, 2007).

Cross sectional studies have suggested that two broad bands of personality, impulsivity/novelty seeking and neuroticism/negative emotionality, are associated with alcoholism. Longitudinal studies have consistently reported that antisocial behaviour and hyperactivity are related to later alcoholism. (Mulder, 2002).

Personality research has, however, continued, and several studies have sought to identify personality characteristics associated with the onset of heavy drinking and other drug use. The results suggest that such use is more common among adolescents and adult population who show pre–drug use signs of one or more of the following: rebelliousness, other adjustment problems, depression, and sensation seeking (Kandel & Yamaguchi, 1985; Stein et al., 1987; Shedler & Block, 1990).

There is evidence for common pre-drinking personality traits in one type of problem drinker. These are people who have alcohol problems from an early age (late teens or early 20s) and strong antisocial tendencies (Allen, 1996; Molina et al., 2002).

Little work has been done in India on the personality factors of alcoholics. These personality factors have a significant effect on treatment outcome. Psychological assessment of 100 consecutive male inpatients alcohol dependents, and an equal number of controls matched for age, sex, occupation and regional background was carried out, State-Trait Anxiety Inventory, Hamilton Rating Scale for Depression, Multiphasic Personality Questionnaire, Maudsley Personality Inventory, Toronto Alexithymia Scale, Self-esteem Inventory and Presumptive Stressful Life Events scale. Alcohol-dependent individuals show significantly high neuroticism, extroversion, anxiety, depression, psychopathic deviation, stressful life events and significantly low self-esteem as compared with normal control subjects (Chaudhury , Das , Ukil,2006).

Zuckerman, Eysenck, (1977) investigated that correlation between personality variables and alcoholism can be obtained because of unrecognized confounds at the measurement on design level, some personality scales contain items that directly reference substance use. As a case in point, disinhibition subscale of the sensation-seeking scale-version V is a frequently employed self-report measure of sensation seeking and impulsivity containing two items that directly asses substance use.(I often like to get high). I feel best after taking a couple of drinks. Failure to address this confounding of item content inflates the magnitude of the correlation between disinhibition and alcohol consumption (Darkes, Greenbaum, & Goldman, 1998).

It is found that personality variables are viewed in the context of mediating and moderating relationship (Miller, 1995).

Personality variables have been posited to mediate the effects of more distal variables, such as family history on outcome (Cloninger, 1987., Sher et al, 2000).

Gustafson(1994) mentioned that people's aggressive tendencies are normally controlled by inhibiting forces. Alcohol would then increase the likelihood of aggressive behavior chemically, through direct pharmacological effects on the brain.

It is found that alcohol contributes indirectly to increased aggression by causing cognitive, emotional, and psychological changes that may reduce self–awareness or result in inaccurate assessment of risks (Bushman, 1997).

It is suggested that alcohol increases aggression because people expect it to do so. The association of alcohol intoxication with aggression would thus be a product of social learning and cultural influences (MacAndrew & Edgerton, 1969; Bandura, 1973; Lang & Stritzke, 1993). Studies show that people act aggressively even if they only believe they have consumed alcohol, as shown by experiments that used placebos (Bushman & Cooper 1990; Gustafson, 1994; Bushman, 1997; Lipsey et al. 1997).

Barnes, (1983) investigated that there are models that view personality characteristics as consequence of alcoholism. Such model assume that the psychosocial (eg. life stress, demoralization) consequences of alcoholism disorder result, either directly or indirectly, in personality changes. There is considerable evidence that the cross-sectional correlates of clinical alcoholism differ from the prospective correlates risk for alcoholism, leading to distinction between pre-alcoholic and clinical alcoholic personalities. Further support for the distinction between pre-alcoholic and clinical alcoholic traits comes from studies comparing changes in personality traits in alcoholics over an extended period of abstinence. Some traits appear stable (especially those related to psychopathic traits). Where as others appear to normalize" especially those related to anxiety and depression.

Sher (1991) explains that the personality variables have been viewed as having only indirect effects on disorders; that is their primary effects are mediated by other variables more proximal to outcome. It has been posited that individuals who are high on trait related to negative affectivity are more likely to experience subjective distress and consequently turn to alcohol for 'self-medication' purposes.

Sher et al suggested that the effect of family history on offspring alcoholism could be mediated by such a multistage chain where family history (a distal variable) is related to behavioral under control (a personality variable) which in turn is related to alcohol outcome expectancies (a proximal variable) which in turn is related to alcohol involvement.

In addition to mediating type relationship, there is ample evidence to suggest that personality can play a moderating role in alcohol use and alcoholism, interacting with various risk factors to exacerbate the likelihood of consumption or disorder; that is, ones relative standing on a personality dimension can determine the strength of relation between a predictor variable and an alcohol related outcome. For example the trait of dispositional self awareness (a personality variable) has been shown to interact with life events (a predictor variable) in determining the likelihood of relapse (Hull & Young, 2005).

Similarly self awareness has been shown to interact with family history of alcoholism in predicting offspring alcohol problems (Rogsch, Chassin & Sher 1990) and appears to moderate the relationship between alcohol outcome expectancies and alcohol use (Bartholaw, & Sher, 2000).

According to Hoffman, Loper, Kammeier, (1974) and Loper, Kammeier, Hoffman, (1973) another approach by them for seeing whether a personality type predisposes the individual to become alcoholic is to take measurements of young people and to see whether a scale predicts which will become alcoholics and which will not. This strategy was employed by a group of Minnesota researchers. They compared the MMPI scores of college students who later became alcoholics with those who did not. The MMPI scores between the two groups showed differences. In the direction of higher sociopathy, defiance of authority, and impulsiveness among those who were to later become alcoholics. Clearly, repeated findings have shown this kind of anti-social impulsiveness to characterize alcoholic males and females both before and after they are clinically diagnosed as alcoholics.

Many studies have shown the importance of personality traits as factors related to alcohol use and misuse. The relationship between personality traits and alcohol consumption was studied in a sample of 149 non-alcoholic women using the Karolinska Scales of Personality (KSP) and the Eysenck Personality Questionnaire-Revised (EPQ-R). The results showed positive correlations between alcohol consumption and dis-inhibitory personality traits (sensation seeking, impulsivity, psychopathy, nonconformity) and dimensions (psychoticism and extraversion). Sensation seeking combined with impulsivity were the strongest predictors of alcohol consumption (Elena & Generós, 1998).

The meta-analysis showed alcohol involvement was associated with low conscientiousness, low agreeableness, and high neuroticism, a personality profile that: a) fits on the low end of a superordinate personality dimension that has been called self-control; and b) makes treatment difficult. Several significant moderators of effect size were found, including the following: studies of individuals in treatment for alcohol problems showed a more negative pattern of personality traits than did other studies; cross sectional studies, but not longitudinal studies, showed a significant effect for agreeableness, perhaps suggesting that low agreeableness may have a different causal link to alcohol involvement (Malouff, Thorsteinsson, Rooke & Schutte, 2007).

Vaillant (1983), discovered that 7 times as many Irish

Americans as Italian Americans and others in his Boston sample became alcoholic. When comparing a group of Harvard students with an inner-city group of white ethnics, he also found more than three times the alcoholism rate among the inner-city group (all these men's drinking histories were followed for over 40 years. There is a heightened tendency to see alcohol both as a salvation and as an evil force that can take control of the individual.

Jessor & Jessor (1977) developed a complex model which takes into account personality, the person's immediate environment, and the larger social groups and values that the individual pursues. According to them, young who are oriented toward achievement or other prosocial activity are unlikely to abuse drugs or alcohol whatever their personality type.

ALCOHOLISM AND HARDINESS

It is found that certain types of people fall ill and have a difficult time overcoming sickness while others seem to be unaffected by illness and can buffer a stressful situation (Florian, Mikulincer, & Taubman, 1995; Hull, Van Treuren, Virnelli, 1987; Kobasa, 1979a; Kobasa, 1979b;Kobasa, Maddi, & Kahn, 1982; Li-Ping Tang & Hammontree, 1988). Selye (1979) defined the concept of stress as the nonspecific response of the body to any demand made upon it. Through experimental data, a direct link has been made between abnormal immune responses and stress. In addition to the stress-disease connection, it seems personality and other mediators are the connection between stressful life events and illness or health.

According to Kobasa (1979a), hardy people are buffered against stressful life situations because they engage in certain affective, cognitive, and behavioral responses. In turn, buffering the stressors leads to better overall health.

Kobasa (1979a) worked with executives working under conditions of stress. Control was measured through four instruments, commitment with the Alienation Test, and challenge with 6 instruments. Kobasa suggests that a hardy personality plays the role of a buffer in the stress-illness relationship. This study was one of the first to significantly correlate the role of personality and other mediators in the connection between stressful life events and illness or health. In this study, Kobasa's results indicated that high stress/low illness executives can be distinguished from high stress/ high illness subjects.

Since Kobasa's 1979a study, many other researchers have investigated the health and hardiness connection (Florian, 1995; Hull, 1987; Kobasa, 1979b; Kobasa et al. 1981; Kobasa et al. 1982; Greene & Nowack, 1995). Greene & Nowack (1995) studied coping styles in relation to hardiness and health and supported the notion that a positive association exists between stress, coping and health. Specifically, hardiness was correlated with four coping styles. In accordance with this finding, Li-Ping Tang & Hammontree (1988) determined hardiness was significantly associated with future strain and stress. Results ultimately showed that "Hardiness will operate as a resistance resource in the stress and strain relationship and also the stress and illness relationship."

Cooper, Cary & Payne, (1991), explored the relationship between certain personality characteristics and coping with stress. Related research by Bruce (1992), discusses coping models, which is mostly a recent phenomenon. Their research presented current models of coping described the coping process, and related the coping process to environmental factors, personal variables, and desirable outcomes.

Someya, & Toshiyuki (1999), investigated the relationship between coping strategies and personality traits. The results indicated that personality traits such as neuroticism were associated with emotional oriented coping in major depressive disorder.

A five-year study, by Kobasa (1982), examined the role of hardiness and its interaction with stressful life events in relation to present health status. Hardiness is shown to be indirectly related to less illness development in the presence of stressful life events, supporting the concept of hardiness as a resistance resource. Testing by Rhodevault and Agustodttir (1984), revealed that hardy individuals report more positive self-statements than low hardy subjects do. Physiologically, high hardy individuals displayed higher levels of systolic blood pressure during the experimental period, indicating more active coping efforts

The effects of hardiness have also been linked to the drug field in regards to coping with addiction. A study conducted by Hirky & Anne, (1998) interviewed injection drug users in an urban methadone program to examine whether coping serves as a mediator of the relationship between social support, personality hardiness, and psychological distress. Results indicated the relationship between hardiness and distress was fully mediated through lower levels of a latent construct measured by behavioral disengagement and denial coping. The path from hardiness to coping was significant, as was the path from coping to distress. Direct effects to distress were found for social support, life events, and gender. Whether stress is a direct result from a biological dependency or social environments, people who exhibit characteristics of a hardy personality will better cope with that stress.

SELF-ESTEEM AND ALCOHOLISM

Consuming alcohol and level of self-esteem have both been shown to be related to a person's mood. In an experiment by McCollam, Burish, Maisto, & Sobell (1980), participants who consumed alcohol reported significantly higher levels of positive affect, such as elation, than sober participants. In addition, sober participants reported being more depressed than intoxicated participants. Similarly, Diener & Emmons (1985) found that self-esteem is also positively correlated with positive affect; participants with higher self-esteem reported being happier and joyful than participants with low selfesteem. These results show that both alcohol

87

intoxication and high self-esteem have the same relationship with mood. Aggression is also shown to be related to intoxication and self-esteem in a similar way. In a meta-analysis of 30 studies, Bushman & Cooper (1990) shows that alcohol actually causes aggressive behavior. Heartherton & Vohs (2000) also found a relationship between self-esteem and aggression. Following a threat to their ego, Alcohol and Self-Esteem 5 participants with high self-esteem showed a significantly higher increase in antagonistic behavior and hostility than participants with low self-esteem. In addition, Kernis, Grannemann, & Barclay (1989) found that instability in self-esteem is a predictor of anger and hostility. This research shows that aggression is related to alcohol intoxication and high self-esteem in the same way.

Studies have found that low self-esteem is the universal common denominator among all people suffering from alcohol addiction. Candito(1996) reports, that those who have identified themselves as "recovered alcoholics" indicate that low self-esteem is the most significant problem in their lives. Candito further reported that low self- esteem is the underlying origin of all problematic behaviors resulting in alcohol abuse. This is also shared by Keegan (1987) who maintains that low self- esteem is either the cause or contributes to maintain alcohol and drug abuse.

Rivas Torres and colleagues (Rivas, Fernandez & Fernandez, 1995) examined the relationship among self-esteem, health values, and health behaviors among adolescents. They found a significant relationship between self-esteem and general health behavior for both younger and older adolescents, and that self-esteem accounted for a significant percent of the variance in mental health behavior, social health behavior, and total health behavior.

Based on the work of Lyons & Chamberlain (1994) expected that self-esteem would mediate the relationship between minor life events and health. They found a direct correlation between self-esteem and health at two time periods in their study.

Bernard, Hutchison, Lavin, & Pennington, (1996) found high correlations among self-esteem, ego strength, hardiness, optimism, and maladjustment, and all of these constructs were significantly related to health.

Self-esteem has long been believed to play an important role in the use of alcohol and psychoactive substances (Charalampous, Ford, & Skinner, 1976; Donnelly, 2000).

Several researchers have argued that low self-esteem poses high risk for substance abuse in some populations, including adolescents, college students (Mitic, 1980; Yanish, & Battle, 1985), young females (Beckman, 1978; Engs, & Hanson, 1989) and African Americans (Grills, & Longshore, 1996). Results of these studies have led researchers to promote the theory that if levels of self-esteem can be determined, it may be possible to predict, change, or improve the lives of some people (Gross 1970; Jessor, & Jessor 1977; Laflin, Moore-

Hirschl, Weis, & Hayes, 1994). The relationship between self-esteem and substance abuse is based on studies that involved alcohol use by students in high school or college, thereby severely limiting the generalizability of findings to more mature populations, such as the chronically homeless substance-abusing men living in urban settings (Segal, Rhenberg, & Sterling, 1975).

Self-esteem has been linked to self and self-will, and has emerged as an important tool for understanding human behavior and for treating negative thoughts, inner feelings of incompleteness, emptiness, self-doubt and self hatred (Adler, Wingert, Houston, Manly, & Cohen, 1992; Crocker, Luthanen, Blaine, & Broadnax, 1994).

Kaplan's (1975) viewed that all individuals possess the "self-esteem motive," directing them toward minimizing negative self-attitudes and maximizing positive perceptions of the self. Low self-esteem and a lack of conformity were found to be high risk factors strongly correlated with the use of tobacco, alcohol and other drugs by young adults (Ward, 2002). Several empirical studies found significant relationships between self-esteem and self-reported problem drinking (Beckman, 1978; Botvin, Schinke, Epstein, Diaz, & Botvin, 1995; Corbin, McNair, & Carter 1996; Glindemann, Scott, & Fortney, 1999; Maney, 1990; Parish, & Parish, 1991; Schaeffer, Schuckit, & Morrissey, 1976).

Mitic (1980) found that regular alcohol drinkers had greater scores for self-esteem compared with heavy drinkers and abstinent adolescents, and that heavy drinking was associated with low self-esteem for females.

Other researchers have found individuals with high levels of self-esteem displayed lower levels of serious involvement with alcohol or illicit drugs and exhibited lower tendency to experiment with either alcohol or illicit drugs (Gorman, 1996; Schroeder, Laflin, & Weis, 1993).

A study involving working-class males in the Metropolitan Los Angeles area found a moderate negative correlation between self-esteem (measured by the Rosenberg 10-item Scale) and a 6-item measure of drinking problems (Seeman, & Seeman, 1992).

In another study, it was investigated that depression and self-esteem both are negatively co-related to alcohol consumption (DeSemone et al, 1994).

Gossop (1976), identified considerable deficiencies in self-esteem among drug-dependent patients, and believes that teenagers with low self-esteem who are exposed to drugs must be considered to be at-risk.

Miller (1988), demonstrated that a program to increase self-esteem significantly changed the attitudes of students regarding their alcohol and drug use.

Glindemann, Geller, & Fortney, (1999) took a slightly different approach than other studies. They used a single party as a basis for the research. Participants completed a self-esteem survey a couple of

91

weeks prior to the party. Their blood alcohol content was measured as the participants exited the party. Their results were consistent with previous studies in regards to self-esteem and alcohol consumption and with no significant differences between the genders.

Similarly, Diener & Emmons (1985), found that self-esteem is also positively correlated with positive affect; participants with higher self-esteem reported being happier and joyful than participants with low self-esteem. These results show that both alcohol intoxication and high self-esteem have the same relationship with mood.

In a study on adolescent drinking behavior, adolescents with high self-esteem reported consuming less alcohol than adolescents with low self esteem and reported smaller increases in alcohol consumption over time (Gerrard, Gibbons, Reis-Bergan, & Russell, 2000).

In addition, in a study on college students, students with low self-esteem became more intoxicated at a fraternity party than students with high-self esteem (Glindemann, Geller, & Fortney, 1999).

Although this research shows a relationship between alcohol and self-esteem, it does not focus on the reverse of this correlation between alcohol and self-esteem; there is little if any evidence that investigates how alcohol abuse influences self-esteem.

Although no direct biological link between alcohol and its influence on self-esteem has been investigated, an indirect relationship between alcohol and self-esteem can be seen by investigating similar effects alcohol and self-esteem have on behavior and cognition. Alcohol affects several neurotransmitters in the human body that influence basic functions such as memory, emotions, arousal, sleep, pain, and response to stress (Chastain, 2006). When alcohol is consumed, the balance of these neurotransmitters in the brain is altered, causing behavioral and cognitive changes involving mood, aggression, social interactions, and risk-taking behavior. Correlations with these behaviors can be seen with both alcohol and self-esteem, showing an indirect relationship between level of alcohol intoxication and self-esteem.

A study done on Self-esteem and gender influence by Mulder, Roger (2002) revealed that self-esteem and gender significantly and independently predicted alcohol-related attitudes, intentions, and follow-up behaviour.

LEARNED HELPLESSNESS AND ALCOHOLISM

The effects of learned helplessness are lack of self confidence, poor problem solving, wandering attention and feeling hopeless. Other symptoms include; difficulty in learning behavior pattern in reaction to controllable adversities, reduced motivation in initiating coping responses and emotional reactions of sadness (Ramirez, Maldonado & Martos, 1992).

Research has also identified strong association between trauma and alcoholism in a sample of Vietnam combat veterans showed signs of alcohol addiction (Bremner, Southwick, Darnell &

Charney, 1996). Similarly women exposed to childhood rape often report turning to alcohol use (Epstein, Saunders, Kilpatric, & Resnick, 1998). In addition to that investigators found that 40% of patients receiving treatment for substance abuse also experienced some of the traumatic incidents (Dansky, Roitzcsh, Brady & Saladin, 1997).

Low personal control and a sense of meaninglessness of life attributes associated with a pattern of human learned helplessness have also been described as contributing to the onset of alcoholism /drug use, as well as the maintenance of chronic substance abuse (Quinless & Nelson, 1988).

Robert & Edward (1996) conducted a study on a sample of 30 consecutive cocaine dependent individuals seeking treatment for the first time. Results indicated that the LHS was internally consistent when administered to this clinical sample and that theoretically meaningful and statistically significant relationships with other measures of psychological functioning were observed. Scores on the LHS were related to treatment retention/outcome.

Thornton et al (2003) studied the pretreatment levels of learned helplessness (LH) related to outcomes for substance-dependent individuals receiving high-structure, behaviorally oriented (HSB) or low-structure, facilitative (LSF) treatment. The subjects were 120 substance-dependent patients randomly assigned to the HSB or the LSF treatment style for up to 12 weeks of weekly individual counseling. The two groups were compared across pretreatment characteristics as well as in-treatment, end-of-treatment, and 9-month postadmission follow-up outcome measures. Outcomes reflected reduction in problem severity, abstinence, retention, dropout rate, and ratings of treatment benefit. Significant and comparable reductions in symptoms occurred for the HSB and LSF patients both during treatment and at follow-up. Comparisons of other outcomes also did not consistently favor either treatment style. However, significant and consistent interactions were observed between LH and treatment styles with respect to several outcome measures, and these effects were independent of pretreatment levels of depression, addiction severity, and readiness for treatment. Specifically, the more helpless patients did significantly better in HSB treatment, whereas the less helpless patients had better outcomes in LSF treatment. A matching approach that assigns patients to high- and low-structure treatments based on pretreatment levels of LH might improve treatment outcomes for substance-dependent patients.

Richard et al (1989) studied the relationship between attributional style and post-traumatic stress disorder in addicted patients in a group of 99 patients seeking treatment for alcohol dependence and/or pathological gambling. Consistent, significant relationships were found between learned helplessness attributional style and a variety of measures of PTSD.

Sitharthan , Michael, Sitharthan , & David (2001) worked on the Alcohol Helplessness Scale and its prediction of depression among problem drinkers. A sample of 98 problem drinkers were selected. Hierarchical multiple regression were used to test the helplessness and self-efficacy moderate or mediate the link between alcohol dependence and depression. Helplessness and self-efficacy both significantly and independently mediated between alcohol dependence and depression.

Kannappan, & Cherian, (1990-94) worked on a sample of 119 alcoholics who attended a day care centre completed the 16 PF questionnaire. Information on religion, occupation, order of birth, duration of drinking etc. was recorded for each subject. Results reveal that they scored high on indicating that they were intelligent, aggressive, impulsive, suspicious, imaginative and radical.

Mohan, Virdi, Paramjit, (1994). Investigated the personality of smokers and drinkers adult 500 subjects comprising an equal number of males and females was administered the Eysneck & Eysneck, 1978. Findings indicate that: (a) both smokers and drinkers scored higher on Extraversion and psychotism, where as non-smokers and non-drinkers scored higher on Neuroticism and lie-scale(LS): (b) Extraversion was found to be positively correlated with smoking as well as drinking; (c) Neuroticism correlated negatively with drinking.

The study compared personality need traits of male and female heroin addicts. It showed that both male and female addicts have a tendency to seek support and affection in time of depression and suffering. Male addicts scored significantly higher on need traits of order, affiliation and change. Similar findings have been reported by Steer & Schut in 1978 who found that addicted males have high needs for dominance, affiliation, exhibition and change.

METHOD AND PROCEDURE

The main purpose of the study was to analyze the relationship between hardiness, self-esteem and learned helplessness with different levels of alcohol use among adult males aged between 25-45 years. The selection of the variables of the present study was done on the basis of a review of related studies done in this field.

HYPOTHESES

1) Increased Level of Alcohol Use will be negatively related to Hardiness and its dimensions i.e. Commitment, Challenge and Control.

2) Increased Level of Alcohol Use will be negatively related to self-esteem.

3) Increased Level of Alcohol Use will be positively related to learned helplessness.

4) There will be significant difference between the three groups Social Drinkers, Problem Drinkers and Alcohol Dependents in relation to Commitment, Challenge and Control.

5) There will be significant difference between the three groups Social Drinkers, Problem Drinkers and Alcohol Dependents in relation to hardiness.

6) There will be significant difference between the three groups Social Drinkers, Problem Drinkers and Alcohol Dependents in relation to Self-esteem.

7) There will be significant difference between the three groups Social

Drinkers, Problem Drinkers and Alcohol Dependents in relation to Learned Helplessness.

8) Hardiness, self-esteem & learned helplessness will significantly contribute to increased Level of Alcohol Use.

TOOLS USED FOR THE PRESENT STUDY

The tools were selected in accordance with the aims and objectives of the study. While selecting the tools, psychometric properties, nature of sample, competence of the investigator in scoring and interpretation was taken into consideration. The scales had to be adapted/translated for the sample of the present study.

The Tools used for the study were as follows:

1) Short Alcohol Dependence Data Questionnaire (Raistrick, Dunbar, & Davidson, 1983).

2) Hardiness Scale (Kobasa & Kahn, 1982).

3) Self-esteem Inventories Adult Form (Coopersmith's, 1981).

4) Learned Helplessness Scale (Dhar, U., Kohli, S, & Dhar, S. 1987).

1. Short Alcohol Dependence Data questionnaire (SADD; Raistrick, Dunbar, &Davidson, 1983). This measure is a 15-item measure that assesses the range of current state alcohol dependence (i.e., behavioral, subjective, and psychobiological changes associated with alcohol dependence). Items were answered by checking off one of the following and scored as follows: never= 0, sometimes=1, often= 2, or nearly always= 3. A 45 is the maximum possible score. Concurrent validity was demonstrated by the SADD's association with the Severity of Alcohol Dependence Questionnaire (SADQ; Stockwell et. al., 1979) of rho=.83, $p>$ .01 (Davidson & Raistrick, 1986). The SADD has evidence of good split-half reliability ($r=$ .87; Raistrick, Dunbar, & Davidson, 1983).

2. Hardiness Scale: To measure the hardiness level of subjects Psychological Hardiness Scale (Kobasa & Kahn, 1982) was used. The scale consists of 12 items positively and negatively keyed covering the important dimensions of hardiness as commitment, control and challenge. The scale was administered to the subjects after translating into Punjabi. Scoring was done in accordance to the manual of the scale. The reliability coefficiant of the translated scale was found to be 0.628 by the investigator. The validity of the scale was also found to be 0.543.

3. Self-esteem Inventories- Adult Form, The scale developed by Coopersmith's(1981) it is uni-dimensional scale which measures the self-esteem level. This form is used with persons aged 16 and above. It consists of 25 items which are to be answered "like me or unlike me". It has both positive and negative items to be answered. Maximum score is 100. High score corresponds to high self-esteem. The author reported its internal consistency reliability (determined by Kuder-Richerdson formula) 0.81 and 0.86. Test-retest reliability reported by author to be 0.88 and 0.70 respectively.

4. Learned Helplessness Scale: (Dhar, U., Kohli, S., & Dhar,

S.,1987). To measure the learned helplessness of subjects the learned helplessness scale was used. This scale consists of 15-items. All items have to be answered in positive, negative and uncertain, and that no statement is to be left out right item was scored as 3, wrong 1 and uncertain as 2. These are designed to have differences in individual reactions to various situations. The scale was administered to the subjects individually as the subjects were not available in groups. Scoring was done as per the manual. The reliability of the scale was determined by two methods (i) The dependability coefficient (Test-Retest) on a sample of 100 subjects is 0.77.(ii) The split half reliability coefficient on a sample of 100 subjects is 0.46 significant at 0.1 level. In order to determine validity from the coefficient of reliability (Garret, 1971), the reliability index was calculated indicated high validity.

SAMPLE

The final sample of the study consisted of 300 adult males. They were in the age group of 25-45 years. This sample was selected out of a larger sample of 500 subjects, so as to have equal numbers of Social Drinkers, Problem Drinkers and Alcohol Dependents belonging to rural and urban areas of Punjab.

Inclusion criteria

1) Age range between 25 to 45 year.
2) Only male subjects.
3) Subjects having adequate reading and writing skill (English or Punjabi).

4) Consistent alcohol consumption since at least 5 years.

Exclusion criteria

1) Concurrent drug use / abuse.

2) A concurrent clinical diagnosis of psychosis, organic brain syndrome or mental retardation.

3) Presence of current or past history of any major medical condition unrelated to alcoholism.

Ethical consideration

1) Informed consent was obtained before the assessment was made.

2) Clients were assured confidentiality.

3) Clients were given the right to opt out of the study.

Figure : 5 Flow chart of the sample of study

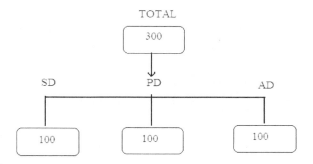

SD- Social Drinkers
PD- Problem Drinkers
AD-Alcohol Dependents

Table-1
SAMPLE CHARACTERISTICS,
(N=300)

		SOCIAL DRINKERS	PROBLEM DRINKERS	ALCOHOL DEPENDENTS
GENDER		MALE, N= 100	MALE, N= 100	MALE, N= 100
AGE-25-30		50%	35%	12%
AGE-31-35		20%	30%	27%
AGE-36-40		18%	17%	32%
AGE-41-45		12%	18%	29%
EDUCATION-	MATRIC	45%	53%	68%
	+2 & ABOVE	55%	47%	32%
LOCALITY-	RURAL	83%	89%	76%
	URBAN	17%	11%	24%

Selection of Subjects

The subjects were divided in three groups i.e. Social Drinkers, Problem Drinkers and Alcohol Dependents on the basis of Short Alcohol Dependence Data Questionnaire (SADD). Equal number of male subjects were chosen for each group. The final sample consisted of 100 Social Drinkers, 100 Problem Drinkers and 100 Alcohol Dependents.

Collection of Data

Local leaders of various communities of Punjab were approached for seeking permission to carry out the proposed research work. After obtaining permission, subjects were contacted and proper rapport was established with the subjects and they were appraised of general objectives of the study and they were assured of confidentiality of the results. In the first phase of the study 500 subjects were administered SADDQ, Self-esteem Inventories, Hardiness Scale and L H Scale. Scoring was done as per the manual. Subjects were classified as Social Drinkers, Problem Drinkers and Alcohol Dependents. 200 subjects were selected in phase one then again subjects were contacted and administered SADDQ, Self-esteem Inventories, Hardiness Scale and L H Scale respectively and 100 more subjects were finally selected. Total 300 subjects were selected dividing them into three groups Social Drinkers, Problem Drinkers and Alcohol Dependents with 100 in each category. Administration and scoring was done as per the respective keys and manuals.

STATISTICAL ANALYSIS

Pearson's correlation was worked out to see the relationship of Hardiness, Self-esteem and Learned Helplessness with different Levels of Alcohol use.

One-way ANOVA was carried out to see the difference between the three groups Social Drinkers, Problem Drinkers and Alcohol Dependents. 't' ratios were also calculated to check the comparison of the three groups.

To check the relative contribution of hardiness, self esteem and learned helplessness on different Levels of Alcohol Use step-wise regression analysis was conducted.

RESULTS AND DISCUSSION

The purpose of the present study is to determine the relationship of Hardiness, Self-esteem and Learned Helplessness with different Levels of Alcohol Use and to determine relative contribution of Hardiness, Self-esteem and Learned Helplessness on different Levels of Alcohol Use.

The present chapter is divided into three sections. In the first section the relationship of Hardiness, Self-esteem and Learned Helplessness with different Levels of Alcohol Use is analyzed/ evaluated/ tested/ checked. In the second section the difference between the three groups Social Drinkers, Problem Drinkers and Alcohol Dependents for Hardiness, Self-esteem and Learned Helplessness is discussed and the third part includes the relative contribution of Hardiness, Self-esteem and Learned Helplessness on different Levels of Alcohol Use.

SECTION- I

To check the relationship of Hardiness, Self-esteem and Learned Helplessness with different Levels of Alcohol Use Pearson's correlation was worked out and the values of correlation are given below in tables 2, 3 and 4.

Table 2
Correlations between Level of Alcohol Use and Hardiness
(N=100)

	Hardiness	Commitment	Challenge	Control
Social Drinker	-0.429*	-0.732*	-0.546*	-0.441*
Problem Drinker	-0.505*	-0.050 (N.S.)	-0.605*	-0.134 (N.S.)
Alcohol Dependent	-0.175**	-0.520*	-0.452*	-0.198**

*Significant at 0.01 level (0.256 for N=100)
** Significant at 0.05 level (0.165 for N=100)
N.S. = Not significant

As evident in table 2 value of correlation between Level of Alcohol Use and Hardiness for Social Drinkers, Problem Drinkers and Alcohol Dependents was found to be -0.429, -0.505 and -0.175 respectively. All these values are negative and statistically significant. Thus the Level of Alcohol Use has significant negative relation with Hardiness for Social Drinkers, Problem Drinkers and Alcohol Dependents. This leads to the acceptance of the hypothesis 1 which states that "Increased Level of Alcohol use will be negatively related to Hardiness and its dimensions i.e. Commitment, Challenge and Control." Shown in Fig. 6, P. No. 96.

According to Kobasa, personality-based hardiness consists of commitment (vs alientation), control (vs powerlessness), and challenge (vs threat). In both retrospective (Kobasa, 1979; Kobasa, 1979a; Kobasa, Maddi, & Puccetti, 1982; Kobasa et al., 1983; Kobasa & Puccetti, 1983; Rhodewalt & Agustsdottir, 1984) and prospective

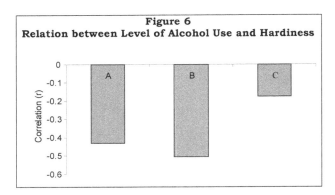

Figure 6
Relation between Level of Alcohol Use and Hardiness

In the figure 6 (Red color shows significant and blue color shows non-significant values)

A- Represents Social Drinkers.
B- Represents Problem Drinkers.
C- Represents Alcohol Dependents.

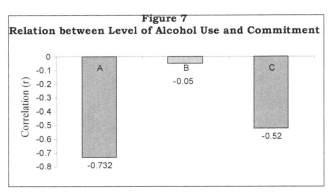

Figure 7
Relation between Level of Alcohol Use and Commitment

In the figure 7 (Red color shows significant and blue color shows non-significant values)

A- Represents Social Drinkers.
B- Represents Problem Drinkers.
C- Represents Alcohol Dependents.

(Kobasa et al., 1981; Kobasa, Maddi, & Kahn, 1982) designs, this factor has emerged as a buffer, significantly decreasing the severity of illness symptoms associated with stressful life events.

Kobasa and her colleagues found that hardiness and stressful life events, respectively decreased and increased illness, and interacted with each other such that hardiness emerged as most effective in periods of high stress (Kobasa et al., 1981; Kobasa, Maddi, & Kahn, 1982).

There are also additive effects such that hardiness in combination with constitutional strengths (Kobasa et al., 1981), is powerful health protector (Kobasa et al., 1983; Rhodewalt & Agustsdottir, 1984). Subjects high in stressful life events but low in illness had greater hardiness scores than subjects in whom similar stressful life event levels were associated with much illness (Kobasa, 1979; Kobasa, Maddi, & Puccetti, 1982; Kobasa et al., 1983; Kobasa & Puccetti, 1983).

The present study shows significant negative relation between Level of Alcohol Use and Hardiness. This may be due to the fact that use of alcohol and other drugs leads to anxiety, fear, depression, loss of will power, poor concentration, feeling useless, moral deterioration and low self confidence. As a result Hardiness, which is referred as a personality style keeps the person healthy even after prolonged exposure to stress. As evident in the present study Hardiness will be associated with alcohol use irrespective of the intensity of the use/

108

abuse. Alcohol use contributes indirectly to increased aggression by causing cognitive, emotional, and psychological changes that may result in inaccurate assessment of risks (Bushman, 1997). This is also mentioned by Gerra, Zaimovic, Moi Gabriele, et al.,(2004) that addicts have high aggression response. However hardy individual exhibits less aggression. Hence, addiction related to aggressive behavior can be controlled by enhancing Hardiness.

Cross sectional studies have suggested that two broad bands of personality, impulsivity/novelty seeking and neuroticism/negative emotionality, are associated with alcoholism. Longitudinal studies have consistently reported that antisocial behaviour and hyperactivity are related to later alcoholism (Mulder & Roger, 2002). Hardiness, which is a positive personality trait has shown negative relationship in our study. Moreover, Control and Commitment components of Hardiness, conceptually may be negatively related to two broad bands of personality described above. Therefore the current results are in the same line as given by Mulder, Roger, (2002).

Personality research has, however, continued, and several studies have sought to identify personality characteristics associated with the onset of heavy drinking and other drug use. The results suggest that such use is more common among adult population who show pre–drug use signs of one or more of the following: rebelliousness, other adjustment problems, depression, and sensation seeking (Kandel & Yamaguchi, 1985; Stein et al., 1987; Shedler &

Block, 1990). Again the dimensions of Hardiness by showing negative significant relationship with various Levels of Alcohol Use in the current study endorse the above mentioned relationship.

There is evidence for common pre-drinking personality traits in problem drinkers (Allen, 1996; Molina et al., 2002). Various studies have provided for predrinking personality traits in addicts. On similar lines the current study makes a case for predrinking enhancement of Hardiness.

Kobasa observed buffering effect of hardiness reflects a personality based inclination to transform, and thereby diminish the stressfulness of life events. The hardy personality style is an amalgam of cognition, emotion, and action aimed at not only survival but also the enrichment of life through development" (Kobasa et al., 1981). Studies have shown positive relation of alcoholism and stressful life events, hence as Hardiness decreases the impact of stressful life situations. It will have a buffering effect for alcohol abuse as well (i.e. Hardiness not only limits alcohol use but also leads to management of stressful life events in a way that they become enriching life experiences.

Kobasa mentioned that hardiness encourages "transformational coping", a dual process of cognition and action, typified in hardy individuals by "optimistic cognitive appraisal (so that the events can be seen in perspective and as not so terrible after all) and decisive interaction with the events, aimed at terminating their stressfulness" (Kobasa et al., 1981).

Within the hardiness perspective (Kobasa, 1982a), transformational coping is "problem specific behaviour that aim at resolving the stressful situation, as well as transforming it into .possibility (i.e. an opportunity for personal growth and the benefit of society)". This mode is distinguished from "regressive coping", by pessimistic appraisal, withdrawal, denial and "attempt(s) to avoid or shrink from the situation". Hence, the proposed mechanism of optimistic cognitive appraisal followed by direct action, is thought to protect the health of hardy persons by transforming the situation, and effectively minimizing the psychological threat of a given stressor. Alcoholics are reported to have a typical style of appraisal as mentioned above by Kobasa. This cognitive style of appraisal can be substituted with the optimistic cognitive appraisal by propagating Hardiness in alcoholism prone individual.

Table 2 also shows that the value of correlation between Level of Alcohol Use and Commitment for Social Drinkers, Problem Drinkers and Alcohol Dependents are -0.732, -0.050 and -0.520 respectively. All these values are negative and significant for Social Drinkers and Alcohol Dependents where as for Problem Drinkers it is not significant. Thus the Level of Alcohol Use has significant negative relation with commitment for Social Drinkers and Alcohol Dependents where as not significantly related to the Level of Alcohol Use among Problem Drinkers. Shown in Fig. 7 P. No. 96.

The commitment disposition is reflected in the hardy person's tendency to involve oneself (rather than experience alienation from) in whatever one is doing or encounters. Committed persons express curiosity about and sense of the meaningfulness of life, and feel an involvement with others that serves as a generalized resistance resource against the impact of stress (Kobasa, 1979). As indicated in this study that Social Drinkers and Alcohol Dependents have strong sense of commitment. As commitment is an ability to recognize one's distinctive values, goals and priorities, and an appreciation of one's capacity to have purpose and to make decisions, committed to self, is seemed essential for the accurate assessment of the threat posed by a particular event, and for the competent handling of it. Committed person's generalized sense of purpose allows them to identify with and find meaningfulness in events, things, and persons of their environment. Investment in self and others is also thought to promote perseverance in the face of stressful life events: "activeness and approach rather than passivity and avoidance." (Kobasa, Maddi & Kahn, 1982).

The present results are in consonance with previous studies as result shows significant negative relation between Level of Alcohol use and Commitment. Commitment is reflected in the ability to feel actively involved with others and a belief in the truth, value and

112

importance of one's self and one's experience (Huang & Wagnitd, 1995; Tartasyky, 1993). Regular use of alcohol reduces the ability of attention and adversely affects the performance. Thus the commitment of those who use alcohol will be lower than those using less alcohol as shown in Social Drinkers in the present study.

Table 2 also shows that the value of correlation between Level of Alcohol Use and Challenge for Social Drinkers, Problem Drinkers and Alcohol Dependents are -0.546, -0.605 and -0.452 respectively. All these values are negative and significant. Thus the Level of Alcohol Use has significant negative relation with Challenge among Problem Drinkers. Shown in Fig. 8, P. No. 105.

Challenge reflects the belief that change is not a threat to personal security, but an opportunity for personal development and growth (Maddi & Kobasa, 1984).

"The challenge disposition is expressed as the belief that change, rather than stability is normal in life and that the anticipation of changes are intering incentives to growth rather than threats to security". (Kobasa, Maddi & Kahn, 1982). The challenge component transform events as stimulating rather than threatening. Challenge is taken not as a threat to personal security but act as cognitive flexibility which allows integration and effective appraisal of the threat of new situations. The active coping style of individuals high in challenge is said to involve transforming oneself and theirby growing rather than conserving and protecting one's former existence.

113

The result of this study shows significant negative relation between Level of Alcohol Use and Challenge. This may be due to the fact that regular alcohol use leads to diminished attention, judgment and control, sensory-motor impairment, Loss of efficiency in finer performance tests, Emotional instability; loss of critical judgment, Disorientation, mental confusion. All these may lead to lower self confidence and as result the ability to accept Challenge is reduced and they accept challenge as a threat to their personal security so the individuals abusing alcohol may continue with alcohol to feel secure and confident in various situations.

Table 2 also shows that the value of correlation between Level of Alcohol Use and Control for Social Drinkers, Problem Drinkers and Alcohol Dependents are -0.441, -0.134 and -0.198 respectively. All these values are negative, for Social Drinkers and Alcohol Dependents these values are significant where as for Problem Drinkers it is not significant. Thus the Level of Alcohol Use has significant negative relation with Control for Social Drinkers and Alcohol Dependents where as not significantly related to the Level of Alcohol Use among Problem Drinkers. Shown in Fig. 9 P. No. 105.

The control disposition is expressed as a tendency to feel and act as if one is influential (rather than powerless and helpless), through the exercise of imagination, knowledge, skill, and choice, in the face of the varied contingencies of life. Control is thought to enhance stress resistance by increasing the likelihood that events will be experienced as a natural outgrowth of one's actions and, therefore, not as foreign, unexpected, and overwhelming experiences (Kobasa, Maddi, & Kahn, 1982). Cognitive control, enables one to interpret, appraise and incorporate various sorts of stressful events into an ongoing life plan and thereby, deactivate their jarring effects. Control also is responsible for the development of a broad and varied repertoire of responses to stress, so that such individuals are capable of autonomously choosing various courses of action to handle the stress.

In this study the result shows significant negative relation between Level of Alcohol Use and Control. This may be due to the fact that regular alcohol use makes the individual dependent, individual become mentally weak and his ability to control himself is reduced.

Chronic heavy drinking often results in poor performance in work or school and inappropriate social behavior. Heavy drinkers often lose the support of family and friends, some of whom may be moderate drinkers. As conflict and disapproval increases at home and at work, many heavy drinkers, feel like they are losing control over their lives. This loss of control often expresses itself as depression. To get relief from depression, the person may drink even more and continue with alcohol use.

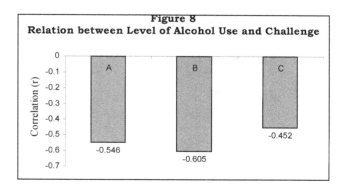

Figure 8
Relation between Level of Alcohol Use and Challenge

In the figure 8 (Red color shows significant values)
A- Represents Social Drinkers.
B- Represents Problem Drinkers.
C- Represents Alcohol Dependents.

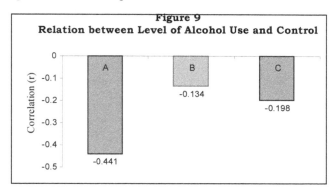

Figure 9
Relation between Level of Alcohol Use and Control

In the figure 9 (Red color shows significant and blue color shows non-significant values)
A- Represents Social Drinkers.
B- Represents Problem Drinkers.
C- Represents Alcohol Dependents.

Table 3
Correlations between Level of Alcohol Use and Self-esteem.
(N= 100)

Sr. No.	Category	Self-esteem
1	Social Drinker	-0.695*
2	Problem Drinker	-0.154 (N.S.)
3	Alcohol Dependent	-0.974*

*Significant at 0.01 level (0.256 for N=100)
** Significant at 0.05 level (0.165 for N=100)
N.S. = Not significant

Table 3 shows that the value of correlation between Level of Alcohol Use and Self-esteem for Social Drinkers, Problem Drinkers and Alcohol Dependents are -0.695, -0.154 and -0.974 respectively. All these values indicate a negative relationship for Social Drinkers and Alcohol Dependents these values are significant where as for Problem Drinkers it is statistically not significant. Thus the Level of Alcohol Use has significant negative relation with Self-esteem for Social Drinkers and Alcohol Dependents where as not significantly related to the Level of Alcohol Use among Problem Drinkers. Hypothesis 2 which states that "Increased Level of Alcohol Use will be negatively related to self-esteem," is thus partially accepted. The hypothesis is accepted for Social Drinkers and Alcohol Dependents but not accepted for Problem Drinkers. Shown in Fig. 10, P. No. 112

Studies have found that low self-esteem is the universal common denominator among all people suffering from alcohol addiction. Candito (1996) reports, that those who have identified themselves as "recovered alcoholics" indicate that low self-esteem is the most significant problem in their lives. Candito further reported that low self- esteem is the underlying origin of all problematic behaviors resulting in alcohol abuse. This is also shared by Keegan (1987) who maintains that low self- esteem is either the cause or contributes to maintain alcohol and drug abuse.

Torres and colleagues (Rivas, Torres, Fernandez & Fernandez, 1995) examined the relationship among self-esteem, health values, and health behaviors among adolescents. They found a significant relationship between self-esteem and general health behavior for both younger and older adolescents, and that self-esteem accounted for a significant percent of the variance in mental health behavior, social health behavior, and total health behavior. Our study indicates that the reverse may also be true; i.e. lower self-esteem associated with increased alcohol use which an indicator of poor mental health behaviour.

Other researchers have found individuals with high levels of self-esteem displayed lower levels of serious involvement with alcohol or illicit drugs and exhibited lower tendency to experiment with either alcohol or illicit drugs (Gorman, 1996; Schroeder, Laflin, & Weis, 1993). Our study indicates that it is true across different Levels of Alcohol Use i.e. in Social Drinkers as well as Alcohol Dependents.

In a study on adolescent drinking behavior, adolescents with high self-esteem reported consuming less alcohol than adolescents with low self esteem and reported smaller increases in alcohol consumption over time (Gerrard, Gibbons, Reis-Bergan, & Russell, 2000). These results are confirmed for the adult sample in our study.

The result shows significant negative relation between Level of Alcohol Use and Self-esteem. This may be due to the fact that low self-esteem and a lack of conformity were found to be high risk factors strongly correlated with the use of tobacco, alcohol and other drugs by young adults (Ward, 2002). Several empirical studies found significant relationships between self-esteem and self-reported problem drinking (Beckman, 1978; Botvin et al., 1995b; Corbin, McNair, & Carter 1996; Glindemann, Scott, & Fortney, 1999; Maney, 1990; Parish, & Parish 1991; Schaeffer, Schuckit, & Morrissey, 1976). While the association of low self-esteem with alcohol use is well established in the literature, our study shows that the results are consistent across Alcohol Dependents at the one end and Social Drinkers at the other end.

Infact, Candito (1996) reports, that those who have identified themselves as "recovered alcoholics" indicate that low self-esteem is the most significant problem in their lives. Thus, even those who learned to control have repeated it to be the most significant factor.

Bravo, Gracia, Fernandez, Carujo(1990) have also found that addicts have a very low self esteem than others.

Smart, Baumeister & Boden, (1994) investgated that alcoholics and drug abusers had lower self esteem.

Table 4

Correlations between Level of Alcohol Use and Learned Helplessness (N=100)

Sr. No.	Category	Learned Helplessness
1	Social Drinkers	0.000 (N.S.)
2	Problem Drinkers	0.024 (N.S.)
3	Alcohol Dependents	0.371*

*Significant at 0.01 level (0.256 for N=100)
** Significant at 0.05 level (0.165 for N=100)
N.S. = Not significant

As evident in table 4 value of correlation between Level of Alcohol Use and Learned Helplessness for Social Drinkers, Problem Drinkers and Alcohol Dependents is found to be 0.000, 0.024 and 0.371 respectively. The values for Social Drinkers and Problem Drinkers are not significant but positive and statistically significant relation was found for Alcohol Dependents. Thus the Level of Alcohol Use has significant positive relation with Learned Helplessness for Alcohol Dependents but no significant relation for Problem Drinkers and for Social Drinkers there is no significant correlation. This leads to the partial rejection of the hypothesis 3 which states that "Increased Level of Alcohol Use will be positively related to learned helplessness." The hypothesis is rejected for Social Drinkers and Problem Drinkers, where as accepted for Alcohol Dependents. Shown in Fig. 11, P. No. 112.

The result shows significant positive relation between Level of Alcohol Use and Learned Helplessness for alcohol dependents. This may be due to the fact that the effects of learned helplessness are lack

120

of self confidence, poor problem solving, wandering attention and feeling hopeless. Other symptoms include; difficulty in learning behavior pattern in reaction to controllable adversities, reduced motivation in initiating coping responses and emotional reactions of sadness (Ramirez, Maldonado & Martos, 1992). As discussed above use of alcohol and other drugs lead to anxiety, fear, depression, loss of will power, poor concentration, feeling useless, moral deterioration and low self confidence. Our study indicates that these factors may be actively involved in the Alcohol Dependents but is not applicable to Social Drinkers and Problem Drinkers.

Research has also identified strong association between trauma and alcoholism in a sample of Vietnam combat veterans showed signs of alcohol addiction (Bremner, Southwick, Darnell & Charney, 1996). Similarly women exposed to childhood rape often report turning to alcohol use (Epstein, Saunders, Kilpatric, & Resnick, 1998). In addition to that investigators found that 40% of patients receiving treatment for substance abuse also experienced some of the traumatic incidents (Dansky, Roitzcsh, Brady & Saladin, 1997). These studies make a case for enhanced chances of being affected by learned helplessness. Some reports indicates that life situations in the lives of alcohol addicted individuals that predispose them to the generation of Learned Helplessness.

Low personal control and a sense of meaninglessness of life attributes associated with a pattern of human learned helplessness have also been described as contributing to the onset of alcoholism /drug use, as well as the maintenance of chronic substance abuse (Quinless & Nelson, 1988). As indicated in our study that the Alcohol Dependents have more scores than Social and Problem Drinkers. Thus Level of Alcohol Use is positively related to Learned Helplessness.

Richard et al (1989) studied the relationship between attributional style and post-traumatic stress disorder in addicted patients in a group of 99 patients seeking treatment for alcohol dependence and/or pathological gambling. Consistent, significant relationships were found between learned helplessness attributional style and a variety of measures of PTSD. Similarly, our study have shown the significant relationship between alcohol use and Learned Helplessness.

Sitharthan , Michael, Hough , Sitharthan , David & Kavanagh (2001) worked on the Alcohol Helplessness Scale and its prediction of depression among problem drinkers. A sample of 98 problem drinkers were selected. Hierarchical multiple regression were used to test the helplessness and self-efficacy moderate or mediate the link between alcohol dependence and depression. Helplessness and self-efficacy both significantly and independently mediated between alcohol dependence and depression. But in the current study the result shows that Hardiness and Self-esteem significantly contribute to increase Level of Alcohol Use for Social Drinkers whereas for Problem Drinkers and Dependents do not significantly contribute for the same.

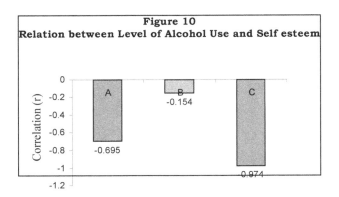

Figure 10
Relation between Level of Alcohol Use and Self esteem

In the figure 10 (Red color shows significant and blue color shows non-significant values)
A- Represents Social Drinkers.
B- Represents Problem Drinkers.
C- Represents Alcohol Dependents.

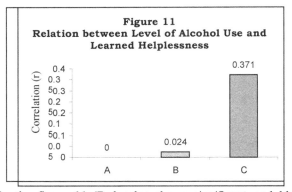

Figure 11
Relation between Level of Alcohol Use and Learned Helplessness

In the figure 11 (Red color shows significant and blue color shows non-significant values)
A- Represents Social Drinkers.
A- Represents Social Drinkers.
B- Represents Problem Drinkers.
C- Represents Alcohol Dependents.

SECTION- II

To study the difference between the three groups Social Drinkers, Problem Drinkers and Alcohol Dependents for hardiness, self-esteem and learned helplessness ANOVA was worked out and the t-ratios were calculated and the values are given in the tables given below:

Table 5
Summaries of Analysis of Variance for Social Drinkers, Problem Drinkers and Alcohol Dependents in relation to Commitment

	Sum of Squares	Degree of freedom	Mean Square	F
Between Groups	1.927	2	0.963	0.777 (N.S.)
Within Groups	368.020	297	1.239	
Total	369.947	299		

N.S. = Not Significant.

Table 5 shows that the value of F is 0.777 which is not significant. Thus there is no significant difference between the three groups Social Drinkers, Problem Drinkers and Alcohol Dependents in relation to Commitment.

The result shows no significant difference in the Commitment of Social Drinkers, Problem Drinkers and Alcohol Dependents. This may be due to the situational factors.

Table 6
Summaries of Analysis of Variance for Social Drinkers, Problem Drinkers and Alcohol Dependents in relation to Challenge

	Sum of Squares	Degree of freedom	Mean Square	F
Between Groups	52.260	2	26.130	13.063*
Within Groups	594.070	297	2.000	
Total	646.330	299		

* Significant at 0.01 level of Significance

Table 6 shows that the value of F is 13.063 which is significant at 0.01 level of significance. Thus there is significant difference between the three groups Social Drinkers, Problem Drinkers and Alcohol Dependents in relation to Challenge. As the value of F-ratio is significant the value of t-ratio was calculated for the Challenge between the three groups Social Drinkers, Problem Drinkers and Alcohol Dependents. The values of the t-ratio are given in the table given below.

Table 7
Comparison of Challenge between Social Drinkers, Problem Drinkers and Alcohol Dependents

	Mean	S.D.	t-ratio
Social Drinkers	1.92	1.3903	4.207*
Problem Drinkers	1.05	1.4521	
Social Drinkers	1.92	1.3903	4.835*
Alcohol Dependents	1.02	1.3997	
Problem Drinkers	1.05	1.4521	0.155
Alcohol Dependents	1.02	1.3997	(N.S.)

*Significant at 0.01 level of significance (2.56)
N.S. means not significant

Table 7 reveals that for Challenge the values of means of Social Drinkers and Problem Drinkers are 1.92 and 1.05 respectively. The value of t-ratio is 4.207 which is significant at 0.01 level, thus the Problem Drinkers have significantly more scores of Challenge than Social Drinkers. For Challenge the values of means of Social Drinkers and Alcohol Dependents are 1.92 and 1.02 respectively. The value of t-ratio is 4.835 which is significant at 0.01 level, Social Drinkers thus have significantly more scores of Challenge than Alcohol Dependents. For Challenge the values of means of Problem Drinkers and Alcohol Dependents are 1.05 and 1.02 respectively. The value of t-ratio is 0.155 which is not significant, thus there is not significant difference in Challenge between Problem Drinkers and Alcohol Dependents. Shown in Fig. 12, P. No. 121.

The "Hardy" Disposition as described by Kobasa (1979; Kobasa et al., 1985; Kobasa & Puccetti, 1983), Hardiness is composed of three component personality characteristics: commitment, control, and challenge. These characteristics are thought to function as a resistance resource in the encounter with stressful life events by facilitating the kind of perception, evaluation, and coping that leads to successful resolution of situations created by these events.

The results show that the mean score of challenge of Alcohol Dependents is less than those of Social Drinkers and Problem Drinkers. This may be due to the fact that as the individual becomes dependent on the alcohol the problems like stress, lack of confidence, low

126

performance, and poor problem solving ability, wandering attention and feeling hopeless become part of life. To cope up with all stressful situations individual may use alcohol as coping strategy and continue with that and becomes dependent(Ramirez, Maldonado & Martos, 1992).

Table 8
Summaries of Analysis of Variance for Social Drinkers, Problem Drinkers and Alcohol Dependents in relation to Control

	Sum of Squares	Degree of freedom	Mean Square	F
Between Groups	54.620	2	27.310	20.457*
Within Groups	396.500	297	1.335	
Total	451.120	299		

* Significant at 0.01 level of Significance

Table 8 shows that the value of F is 20.457 which is significant at 0.01 level of significance. Thus there is significant difference between the three groups Social Drinkers, Problem Drinkers and Alcohol Dependents in relation to Control. As the value of F-ratio is significant the value of t-ratio was calculated for the Control between the three groups Social Drinkers, Problem Drinkers and Alcohol Dependents. The values of the t-ratio are given in the table given below. Shown in Fig. 13, P. No. 122.

Table 9
Comparison of Control between Social Drinkers, Problem Drinkers and Alcohol Dependents

	Mean	S.D.	t-ratio
Social Drinkers	-0.15	0.9886	2.83*
Problem Drinkers	-0.58	1.1475	
Social Drinkers	-0.15	0.9886	5.681*
Alcohol Dependents	-1.19	1.3081	
Problem Drinkers	-0.58	1.1475	3.871*
Alcohol Dependents	-1.19	1.3081	

*Significant at 0.01 level of significance (2.56)

Table 9 reveals that for Control the values of means of Social Drinkers and Problem Drinkers are -0.15 and -0.58 respectively. The value of t-ratio is 2.83 which is significant at 0.01 level, thus the Social Drinkers have significantly more scores of Control. For Control the values of means of Social Drinkers and Alcohol Dependents are -0.15 and -1.19 respectively. The value of t-ratio is 5.681 which is significant at 0.01 level, Social Drinkers have significantly more scores of Control. For Control the values of means of Problem Drinkers and Alcohol Dependents are -0.58 and -1.19 respectively. The value of t-ratio is 3.871 which is significant at 0.01 level, the Problem Drinkers have significantly more scores of Control.

This leads to the acceptance of the hypothesis 4 which states that "There will be significant difference between the three groups Social Drinkers, Problem Drinkers and Dependents in relation to Commitment, Challenge and Control".

The results show that the mean score of control of alcohol dependents is less than those of Social Drinkers and Problem Drinkers. This may be due to the fact that as the individual becomes dependent on the alcohol the problems like lack of confidence, and poor problem solving ability, low risk taking ability and feeling hopelessness worsen. According to Bandura (1969) individuals who are subjected to stressful situations may obtain relief from stress through drinking alcohol due to its pharmacological effects. The behavior of drinking is reinforced by the reduction of unpleasant

128

experiences that follows from it. Repeated experiences in which the drinking of alcohol leads to a reduction of anxiety, stress or other aversive stimuli results in a progressive strengthening of the alcohol habits.

Table 10
Summaries of Analysis of Variance for Social Drinkers, Problem Drinkers and Alcohol Dependents in relation to Hardiness

	Sum of Squares	Degree of freedom	Mean Square	F
Between Groups	189.487	2	94.743	29.161*
Within Groups	964.950	297	3.249	
Total	1154.437	299		

* Significant at 0.01 level of Significance

Table 10 reveals that the value of F is 29.161 which is significant at 0.01 level of significance. Thus there is significant difference between the three groups Social Drinkers, Problem Drinkers and Alcohol Dependents in relation to Hardiness. As the value of F-ratio is significant the value of t-ratio was calculated for the Hardiness between the three groups Social Drinkers, Problem Drinkers and Alcohol Dependents. The values of the t-ratio are given in the table given below.

Table 11
Comparison of Hardiness between Social Drinkers, Problem Drinkers and Alcohol Dependents

	Mean	S.D.	t-ratio
Social Drinkers	2.06	1.6503	4.48*
Problem Drinkers	0.95	1.7487	
Social Drinkers	2.06	1.6503	7.069*
Alcohol Dependents	0.12	1.9913	
Problem Drinkers	0.95	1.7487	3.259*
Alcohol Dependents	0.12	1.9913	

*Significant at 0.01 level of significance (2.56)
** Significant at 0.05 level of significance (1.98)
N.S. means not significant

Table 11 reveals that for Hardiness the values of means of Social Drinkers and Problem Drinkers are 2.06 and 0.95 respectively. The value of t-ratio is 4.48 which is significant at 0.01 level, thus the Social Drinkers have significantly more scores of Hardiness than Problem Drinkers. For Hardiness the values of means of Social Drinkers and Alcohol Dependents are 2.06 and 0.12 respectively. The value of t-ratio is 7.069 which is significant at 0.01 level, Social Drinkers have significantly more scores of Hardiness than Alcohol Dependents. For Hardiness the values of means of Problem Drinkers and Alcohol Dependents are 0.95 and 0.12 respectively. The value of t-ratio is 3.259 which is significant at 0.01 level, the Problem Drinkers have significantly more scores of Hardiness than Alcohol Dependents. This leads to acceptance of hypothesis 5 which states that "There will be significant difference between the three groups Social Drinkers,

Problem Drinkers and Alcohol Dependents in relation to Hardiness". Shown in Fig. 14, P. No. 122.

The manner in which the three components of hardiness are seen to interact in facilitating adaptive, transformational (as opposed to regressive) coping is illustrated in the following example of a man faced with being fired from work: the hardy person might not only try to have the decision reverse or look for another job (control) but also interview peers and supervisors in an attempt to get more information about what happened (commitment). Faced with the same event, a person low in hardiness might be indecisive about what to do (powerless), try through distraction to avoid thinking about what happened (alienation) and consider the situation an unequivocal reversal (threat) (Kobasa et al., 1981). Similarly in the context of an individual using or abusing alcohol faced with the same event may be indecisive, powerless, alienation, and consider the situation an unequivocal reversal.

The results show that the mean score of Hardiness of Alcohol Dependents is significantly less as compared to that of Social Drinkers and Problem Drinkers. This may be due to the fact that the general drug use may increase an individual's risk for specific health problems later in life by causing a decrease in physical hardiness during young adulthood (Arria, Amelia, Tarter, Ralph, Thiel & David, 1991).

Consistent with Kobasa's formulation regarding the transformation of stressful life events, high hardy individuals were more likely than low hardy individuals to perceive life events as being desirable or positive and to report that these life events are under their control. It appears that one aspect of hardy individuals' stress resiliency is attributable to their propensity to interpret situations in less stressful ways (Rhodewalt & Agustsdottir, 1984). In the context of our research findings that alcoholics feel powerless when confront with stressful life event and they try to avoid the same.

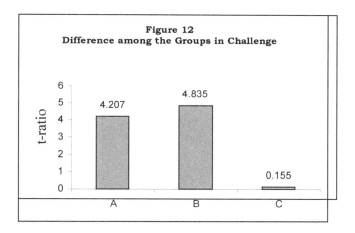

Figure 12
Difference among the Groups in Challenge

In the figure 12 (Red color shows significant and blue color shows non-significant values)
 A- Represents Social Drinkers & Problem Drinkers.
 B- Represents Social Drinkers & Alcohol Dependents.
 C- Represents Problem Drinkers & Alcohol Dependents.

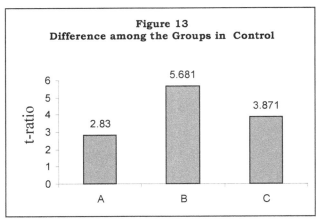

Figure 13
Difference among the Groups in Control

In the figure 13 (Red color shows significant values)
A- Represents Social Drinkers & Problem Drinkers.
B- Represents Social Drinkers & Alcohol Dependents.
C- Represents Problem Drinkers & Alcohol Dependents.

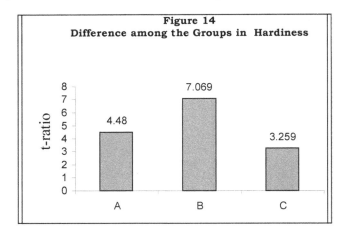

Figure 14
Difference among the Groups in Hardiness

In the figure 14 (Red color shows significant values)
A- Represents Social Drinkers & Problem Drinkers.
B- Represents Social Drinkers & Alcohol Dependents.
C- Represents Problem Drinkers & Alcohol Dependents.

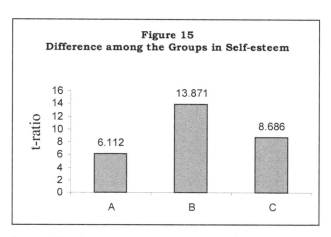

Figure 15
Difference among the Groups in Self-esteem

In the figure 15 (Red color shows significant values)
A- Represents Social Drinkers & Problem Drinkers.
B- Represents Social Drinkers & Alcohol Dependents.
C- Represents Problem Drinkers & Alcohol Dependents.

Table 12
Summaries of Analysis of Variance for Social Drinkers, Problem Drinkers and Alcohol Dependents in relation to Self-esteem

	Sum of Squares	Degree of freedom	Mean Square	F
Between Groups	58912.827	2	29456.413	120.244*
Within Groups	72756.760	297	244.972	
Total	131669.587	299		

* Significant at 0.01 level of Significance

Table 12 reveals that the value of F is 120.244 which is significant at 0.01 level of significance. Thus there is significant difference between the three groups Social Drinkers, Problem Drinkers and Alcohol Dependents in relation to Self-esteem. As the value of F-ratio is significant the value of t-ratio was calculated for the Self-esteem between the three groups Social Drinkers, Problem Drinkers and Alcohol Dependents. The values of the t-ratio are given in the table given below.

Table 13
Comparison of Self-esteem between Social Drinkers, Problem Drinkers and Alcohol Dependents

	Mean	S.D.	t-ratio
Social Drinkers	66.28	12.855	6.112*
Problem Drinkers	54.98	13.755	
Social Drinkers	66.28	12.855	13.871*
Alcohol Dependents	32.56	19.505	
Problem Drinkers	54.98	13.755	8.686*
Alcohol Dependents	32.56	19.505	

*Significant at 0.01 level of significance (2.56)

Table 13 reveals that for Self-esteem the values of means of Social Drinkers and Problem Drinkers are 66.28 and 54.98 respectively. The value of t-ratio is 6.112 which is significant at 0.01 level, thus the Social Drinkers have significantly more scores of Self-esteem. For Self-esteem the values of means of Social Drinkers and Alcohol Dependents are 66.28 and 32.56 respectively. The value of t-ratio is 13.871 which is significant at 0.01 level, the Social Drinkers have significantly more scores of Self-esteem. For Self-esteem the values of means of Problem Drinkers and Alcohol Dependents are 54.98 and 32.56 respectively. The value of t-ratio is 8.686 which is significant at 0.01 level, the Problem Drinkers have significantly more scores of Self-esteem. It can thus be concluded on the basis of above

135

discussion that there is significant difference in the Self-esteem of Social Drinkers and Problem Drinkers, Social Drinkers and Alcohol Dependents, Problem Drinkers and Alcohol Dependents. Thus hypothesis 6 which states that "There will be significant difference between the three groups Social Drinkers, Problem Drinkers and Dependents in relation to Self-esteem" is accepted. Shown in Fig. 15, P. No. 123.

The result again show that mean scores of Self-esteem of alcohol dependents is significantly low as compared to Social Drinkers and Problem Drinkers. This may be due to the fact that the Dependents use of alcohol can further damage self esteem. Alcoholism or addiction can lead to social isolation, or uncontrolled behaviour, alienating those around and may be removing any possible positive feedback (Hunt & Tobin, 2007).

Table 14
Summaries of Analysis of Variance for Social Drinkers, Problem Drinkers and Alcohol Dependents in relation to Learned Helplessness

	Sum of Squares	Degree of freedom	Mean Square	F
Between Groups	6347.127	2	3173.563	56.782*
Within Groups	16599.470	297	55.890	
Total	22946.597	299		

*Significant at 0.01 level of Significance

Table 14 shows that the value of F is 56.785 which is significant at 0.01 level of significance. Thus there is significant difference between the three groups Social Drinkers, Problem Drinkers and

136

Alcohol Dependents in relation to Learned Helplessness. As the value of F-ratio is significant the value of t-ratio was calculated for the Learned Helplessness between the three groups Social Drinkers, Problem Drinkers and Alcohol Dependents. The values of the t-ratio are given in the table given below.

Table 15
Comparison of Learned Helplessness between Social Drinkers, Problem Drinkers and Alcohol Dependents.

	Mean	S.D.	t-ratio
Social Drinkers	28.29	8.8447	-1.29
Problem Drinkers	29.66	6.5137	(N.S.)
Social Drinkers	28.29	8.8447	-10.21*
Alcohol Dependents	38.66	6.8567	
Problem Drinkers	29.66	6.5137	-9.02*
Alcohol Dependents	38.66	6.8567	

*Significant at 0.01 level of significance (2.56)
N.S. means not significant

Table 15 reveals that for Learned Helplessness the values of means of Social Drinkers and Problem Drinkers are 28.29 and 29.66 respectively. The value of t-ratio is -1.29 which is not significant, thus there is no significant difference in the Learned Helplessness of Social Drinkers and Problem Drinkers. For Learned Helplessness the values of means of Social Drinkers and Alcohol Dependents are 28.29 and 38.66 respectively. The value of t-ratio is -10.21 which is significant at 0.01 level, the Alcohol Dependents have significantly more scores of Learned Helplessness. For Learned Helplessness the values of means of Problem Drinkers and Alcohol Dependents are 29.66 and 38.66 respectively. The value of t-ratio is -9.02 which is significant at 0.01

level, the Alcohol Dependents have significantly more scores of Learned Helplessness. It can thus be concluded on the basis of above discussion that the Learned Helplessness of Alcohol Dependents is significantly more as compared to Social Drinkers and Problem Drinkers. The hypothesis 7 which states that "There will be significant difference between the three groups Social Drinkers, Problem Drinkers and Dependents in relation to Learned Helplessness", is thus accepted. Shown in Fig. 16, P. No. 128.

After a traumatic event people often report using alcohol to relieve their symptoms of anxiety, irritability and depression. Alcohol may relieve these symptoms because drinking compensates for defficiencies in endorphin activity following a traumatic experience. With in minutes of exposure to a traumatic event there is an increase in the level of endorphins in the brain. During the time of trauma endorphin level is increased and remains elevated so that the individual remains numb from the emotional and physical pain of the trauma. However, after the trauma is over the endorphin level generally decreases and this may lead to a period of endorphin withdrawal that can last from hours to days. This period of endorphin withdrawal may produce emotional distress and contribute to other symptoms like post traumatic stress disorder. Because alcohol use increases endorphin activity, drinking following trauma may be used to compensate this endorphin withdrawal and thus avoid the associated emotional distress (Volpicelli, Ulm, & Hopson, 1990).

The results of the current study show that the mean score of Learned Helplessness of alcohol dependents is significantly more as compared to that of Social Drinkers and Problem Drinkers. This may be due to the fact that the Level of Alcohol Use by alcohol dependent is positively and significantly related to learned helplessness (table 4).

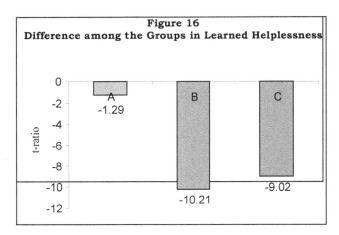

Figure 16
Difference among the Groups in Learned Helplessness

In the figure 16 (Red color shows significant and blue color shows non-significant values)
A- Represents Social Drinkers & Problem Drinkers.
B- Represents Social Drinkers & Alcohol Dependents.
C- Represents Problem Drinkers & Alcohol Dependents.

SECTION- III

To check the causation of hardiness, self esteem and learned helplessness on different Levels of Alcohol Use stepwise regression analysis, R^2 and R along with F were calculated and the values are given in the tables 16, 17 and 18 below.

Table 16
Stepwise Regression Analysis for Social Drinkers

Predictor Variable/s	Degree of Freedom	R^2	R	F
Model I				
Learned Helplessness	99	0.180	0.424	21.488*
Learned Helplessness + Self-esteem	98	0.226	0.476	14.186*
Learned Helplessness + Self-esteem + Hardiness	97	0.188	0.434	9.901*
Model II				
Self-esteem	99	0.002	0.039	0.153
Self-esteem + Hardiness	98	0.007	0.084	0.342
Learned Helplessness + Self-esteem + Hardiness	97	0.188	0.434	9.901*
Model III				
Hardiness	99	0.006	0.080	0.630
Learned Helplessness + Hardiness	98	0.197	0.444	11.927*
Learned Helplessness + Self-esteem + Hardiness	97	0.188	0.434	9.901*

*Significant at 0.01 level
** Significant at 0.05 level

Model I, II and III of Table 16 reveals that for Social Drinkers values of R^2 of Learned Helplessness, Self-esteem and Hardiness are 0.180, 0.002 and 0.006 respectively. 18% of Alcohol use is thus

140

predicted by Learned Helplessness, 0.2% by Self-esteem and 0.6% by Hardiness. The value of R^2 for Learned Helplessness, Self-esteem and Hardiness taken together is 0.188, thus 18.8% of Alcohol use is predicted by Learned Helplessness, Self-esteem and Hardiness taken together. The F value for the conjoint R^2 is 9.901 which is significant at 0.01 level of significance. This leads to the conclusion that Learned Helplessness, Self-esteem and Hardiness conjointly predict Alcohol use among Social Drinkers more as compared to their separate prediction.

Table 17
Stepwise Regression Analysis for Problem Drinkers

Predictor Variable/s	Degree of Freedom	R^2	R	F
Model I				
Learned Helplessness	99	0.051	0.226	5.255**
Learned Helplessness + Self-esteem	98	0.052	0.229	2.684
Learned Helplessness + Self-esteem + Hardiness	97	0.073	0.27	1.781
Model II				
Self-esteem	99	0.021	0.144	2.062
Self-esteem + Hardiness	98	0.021	0.144	1.027
Learned Helplessness + Self-esteem + Hardiness	97	0.073	0.27	1.781
Model III				
Hardiness	99	0.001	0.025	0.061
Learned Helplessness + Hardiness	98	0.051	0.226	2.605
Learned Helplessness + Self-esteem + Hardiness	97	0.073	0.27	1.781

*Significant at 0.01 level
** Significant at 0.05 level

Model I, II and III of Table 17 reveals that for Problem Drinkers values of R^2 of Learned Helplessness, Self-esteem and Hardiness are 0.051, 0.021 and 0.001 respectively. 5.1% of Alcohol use is thus predicted by Learned Helplessness, 2.1% by Self-esteem and 0.1% by Hardiness. The value of R^2 for Learned Helplessness, Self-esteem and Hardiness taken together is 0.073, thus 7.3% of Alcohol use is predicted by Learned Helplessness, Self-esteem and Hardiness taken together. The F value for the conjoint R^2 is 1.781 which is not significant. This leads to the conclusion that Learned Helplessness, Self-esteem and Hardiness conjointly do not predict Alcohol use among Problem Drinkers more as compared to their separate prediction.

Table 18
Stepwise Regression Analysis for Alcohol Dependents

Predictor Variable/s	Degree of Freedom	R^2	R	F
Model I				
Learned Helplessness	99	0.008	0.090	0.807
Learned Helplessness + Self-esteem	98	0.018	0.133	0.872*
Learned Helplessness + Self-esteem + Hardiness	97	0.04	0.2	1.510
Model II				
Self-esteem	99	0.000	0.003	0.001
Self-esteem + Hardiness	98	0.033	0.182	1.653
Learned Helplessness + Self-esteem + Hardiness	97	0.04	0.2	1.510
Model III				
Hardiness	99	0.032	0.172	3.234
Learned Helplessness + Hardiness	98	0.035	0.187	1.759
Learned Helplessness + Self-esteem + Hardiness	97	0.04	0.2	1.510

*Significant at 0.01 level
** Significant at 0.05 level

142

Model I, II and III of Table 18 reveals that for Alcohol Dependents values of R^2 of Learned Helplessness, Self-esteem and Hardiness are 0.008, 0.000 and 0.032 respectively. 0.8% of Alcohol use is thus predicted by Learned Helplessness, 0.000% by Self-esteem and 3.2% by Hardiness. The value of R^2 for Learned Helplessness, Self-esteem and Hardiness taken together is 0.04, thus 4% of Alcohol use is predicted by Learned Helplessness, Self-esteem and Hardiness taken together. The F value for the conjoint R^2 is 1.510 which is not significant. This leads to the conclusion that Learned Helplessness, Self-esteem and Hardiness conjointly do not predict alcohol use among Alcohol Dependents more as compared to their separate prediction.

On the basis of tables 16, 17 and 18 it can be concluded that hypothesis 8 which states that "Hardiness, self-esteem & learned helplessness will significantly contribute to Level of Alcohol Use," is partially rejected. The hypothesis is accepted for Social Drinkers where as rejected for Problem Drinkers and Alcohol Dependents.

The result shows that for Problem Drinkers and Alcohol Dependents- Hardiness, Self-esteem & Learned Helplessness do not significantly contribute to Level of Alcohol Use, where as for Social Drinkers- Hardiness, Self-esteem & Learned Helplessness significantly contribute to Level of Alcohol Use. This may be due to the fact that some values of correlation calculated and given in tables 2, 3 and 4 are not significant. Shown in Fig. Nos. 17, 18, 19 P. No. 133, 134 .

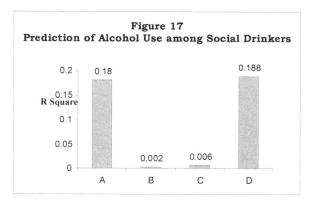

Figure 17
Prediction of Alcohol Use among Social Drinkers

In the figure 17

A- Represents prediction of Level of Alcohol Use by Learned Helplessness.

B- Represents prediction of Level of Alcohol Use by Self-esteem.

C- Represents prediction of Level of Alcohol Use by Hardiness.

D- Represents conjoint prediction of Level of Alcohol Use by Learned Helplessness, Self-esteem and Hardiness.

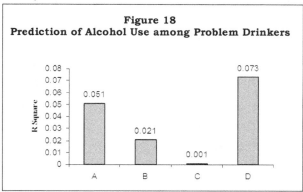

Figure 18
Prediction of Alcohol Use among Problem Drinkers

In the figure 18

A- Represents prediction of Level of Alcohol Use by Learned Helplessness.

B- Represents prediction of Level of Alcohol Use by Self-esteem.

C- Represents prediction of Level of Alcohol Use by Hardiness.

D- Represents conjoint prediction of Level of Alcohol Use by Learned Helplessness, Self-esteem and Hardiness.

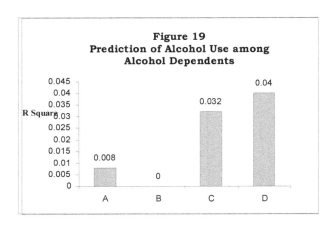

Figure 19
Prediction of Alcohol Use among Alcohol Dependents

In the figure 19
A- Represents prediction of Level of Alcohol Use by Learned Helplessness.
B- Represents prediction of Level of Alcohol Use by Self-esteem.
C- Represents prediction of Level of Alcohol Use by Hardiness.
D- Represents conjoint prediction of Level of Alcohol Use by Learned Helplessness, Self-esteem and Hardiness.

CONCLUSION AND IMPLICATIONS

The results of the present study support the fact that Personality plays an important role in causing alcoholism. Over the past 50 years, hundreds of studies have examined the personality correlates of alcoholics, many of these in search of so-called "Alcoholic Personality" (Sutherland & Tordella, 1950) that was thought to underlie alcoholic behavior. In the first edition of the American Psychiatric Association (APA, 1952) alcoholism was considered a form of personality disorder, implying that disordered personality functioning is a core component of alcoholism.

By the year 1980's, the alcohol research committee came to recognize that, although there was no single constellation of personality traits that was unique to alcoholics, personality measures could be used to distinguish clinical alcoholics(i.e. individual seeking treatment for alcoholism or individual meeting diagnostic criteria for alcoholism) from various comparison groups.

In this study the relationship of Hardiness and Self-esteem are negative whereas the Learned Helplessness is positively related with alcoholism. As the present study shows significant negative relation between Level of Alcohol Use and Hardiness. This may be due to the fact that use of Alcohol and other drugs leads to anxiety, fear, depression, loss of will power, poor concentration, feeling useless, moral deterioration and low self confidence. As a result Hardiness, which is referred as a personality style keeps the person healthy even

146

after prolonged exposure to stress. As evident in the present study Hardiness will be associated with alcohol use irrespective of the intensity of the use / abuse. Alcohol use contributes indirectly to increased aggression by causing cognitive, emotional, and psychological changes that may result in inaccurate assessment of risks (Bushman, 1997). This is also mentioned by Gerra, Zaimovic, Moi Gabriele, et al.,(2004) that addicts have high aggression response. However hardy individual exhibits less aggression. Hence, addiction related to aggressive behavior can be controlled by enhancing Hardiness.

The study showed significant relationship between increased Level of Alcohol Use and Hardiness as a whole for the three groups; Social Drinkers, Problem Drinkers and Alcohol Dependents, so the need is felt by the investigator for these groups that some training programmes can be planned to enhance the Hardiness for the above groups at different levels in clinical settings and in community which can help them to improve their Hardiness and it will ultimately reduce the Level of Alcohol Use. As in this study we have found that the Alcohol Dependents are low hardy than Social Drinkers and Problem Drinkers. Similarly, the Hardiness training can also help the Social Drinkers not to become Alcohol Dependents in future.

Studies have found that low Self-esteem is the universal common denominator among all people suffering from alcohol addiction. Candito (1996) reports, that those who have identified

147

themselves as "recovered alcoholics" indicate that low Self-esteem is the most significant problem in their lives. Candito further reported that low self- esteem is the underlying origin of all problematic behaviors resulting in alcohol abuse. This is also shared by Keegan (1987) who maintains that low self- esteem is either the cause or contributes to maintain alcohol and drug abuse. Several empirical studies found significant relationships between Self-esteem and self-reported problem drinking.

As yielded from the results of this study that the Level of Alcohol Use has significant negative relation with Self-esteem for Social Drinkers and Alcohol Dependents where as not significantly related to the Level of Alcohol Use among Problem Drinkers.

Our findings have shown that Alcohol Dependents have lower Self-esteem than Social Drinkers. Although in Problem Drinkers the relationship was found also negative in nature. So all the three groups need the training to boost their Self-esteem which ultimately help them for controlled drinking. Counseling programmes can be planned on the basis of the present results to raise the level of Self-esteem of Social Drinkers as well as Alcohol Dependents. Health education programmes at different level can be a great help to raise the Self-esteem of the general population which can prevent the onset of alcoholism. In addition to that services can be arranged in de-addiction centers to raise the Self-esteem of alcoholics that can help them to overcome this problem.

Further the results of the present study showed that significant positive relation between Learned Helplessness and Level of Alcohol Use for the three groups. Alcohol Dependents were significantly higher on Learned Helplessness and significantly lower on Self-esteem and Hardiness as compared to Social Drinkers and Problem Drinkers. On the basis of above findings, counseling services can be arranged for Alcohol Dependents in clinical setting as well as in the community to reduce their Learned Helplessness by giving health education and training as the Dependents shown more Learned Helplessness than other two groups. They need to reduce their Learned Helplessness which can help them for controlled drinking.

As our findings concluded that Hardiness, Self-esteem and Learned Helplessness contribute significantly for Social Drinkers. So health education programme can be launched at different level for social drinkers in different societies to help them not to become alcohol dependents in their later life.

LIMITATIONS OF THE STUDY

Some of the limitations in the present study are presented below:

1) The present investigation focused on the adult population only.

2) The present study was confined only to the male subjects.

3) The present study was done in Punjab state only.

4) The role of sociodemographic variables was not included in the study.

RECOMMENDATIONS

On the basis of the findings of present investigation, the following suggestions can be made for future research.

1) Comparative study on Level of Alcohol Use and Hardiness for males and females can be done.

2) Impact of Hardiness, Self-esteem and Learned Helplessness on different Level of Alcohol Use can be explored in general population.

3) Replication of the present study findings need to be done in different age groups.

4) The findings of the present study can be used for future research on substance abuse/alcoholism.

5) Comparative study can be done on alcoholics and non-alcoholics in relation to Hardiness, Self-esteem and Learned Helplessness.

SUMMARY

Alcoholism is a road often traveled yet there is no light at the end. The road only leads to a life of depression, anxiety, anger, stress, and much more. These are all common unwanted personality traits that we experience at one time or another. However, alcoholics exhibit these traits nearly doubled when alcohol is involved. Alcohol inhibits not only our daily bodily functions but our mind as well. Alcoholism leads to withdrawal, low self-esteem, and an overall unwillingness to be a part of society. It can turn the gentle person into a psychopath without knowing it or if they do know, they refuse to admit it. Alcoholism manipulates the way we think and the way we react in common everyday situations. Minor problems are blown out of proportion while major problems are faced with anger, resentment, and often physical force. Alcoholism does nothing positive for an individual. It has many harmful effects and their effect on one's personality is one of the most harmful of all.

Alcoholism and drug abuse is widely recognized as a serious problem world over with severe psychological, social and physical consequences. Hence the problem of drug and alcohol abuse is not unique either to India or to present times (Sachene, 1990) but is a chronic menace.

The health care system is greatly affected by alcoholism. In India, 10% of adults entering private physician's clinics are alcoholics and 15-40% of adult admissions to general hospitals are for alcohol related problems. (W.H.A. Report, 2002). One fact comes to the forefront while analyzing the whole scenario that is what makes certain drinkers strictly remain social drinkers while others further deteriorate to drinking as a habit and become addicts/dependents.

DSM IV-TR (A.P.A., 2005) differentiates different levels of alcohol use as follows: -

Alcohol dependence is characterized by at least three of specific signs or symptoms from inability to control the amount consumed interferences with work, school or social activities, tolerance, withdrawal and duration of problem being at least for a month.

Problem drinkers: These are people who can not drink in a controlled manner, or people whose drinking at one time has adversely affected their health or caused them any economic, professional, legal or personal problems (National Institute on Alcohol Abuse & Alcoholism, 1992).

Social drinking: can be defined as drinking pattern that is found to be acceptable to the society in which they occurs on an infrequent basis during social occasions that may call for alcohol to be present and/or consumed. Those individuals who engage in social drinking generally only have one or two drinks and are easily able to stop drinking at that time. Social drinking is defined as such because under normal circumstances, the individual would probably not choose to consume alcohol but may do so only due to the social situation (United State Department of Health and Human Services, 1992).

Being a resident of Punjab and having worked in various de-addiction centers, I have confronted problems through various young patients tend to fall and their relapse rate is high directly influencing general and psychological well being of their respective families. The subject himself suffers from a range of allied problems ranging from accidental traumas to more specific diseases like mental disorders and liver diseases. In this study the researcher aims to understand/establish the proportionality between the alcohol intake with different characteristics of personality in terms of hardiness, conceptualization of acceptance and regard for one self in terms of self-esteem and the feelings of not having any effective control over life events in terms of learned helplessness.

The primary focus of the research is to aid counseling and de-addiction of the subjects as well as education of the affected families through a scientifically proven approach which would include hardiness, self-esteem, learned helplessness and their relation with different levels of alcohol use.

Research suggests that certain personality factors/traits may play an important role in both the development and maintenance of alcohol dependence (Barnes, 1980). Characteristics that have been identified include impulsivity, negative self concept, weak ego, low social conformity, neuroticism and introversion. It has also been associated with antisocial personality and depressive response styles (Leigh, 1985). This may be explained by the inability of an individual with antisocial personality to anticipate the aversive consequences of his or her behavior. It is likely that in an effort on the part of that person to manage negative emotional evaluations, he may indulge in substance abuse. Further it may be an impulsive act towards anxiety relief. Achievement of relief then provides the positive reinforcement to continue abusing the substance.

HARDINESS

The term hardiness was introduced by Kobasa (1979) to refer to the personality style which keeps the person healthy even after prolonged exposure to stress. Hardy people are hypothesized to possess three general characteristics: commitment, control & challenge.

Commitment- Hardy people show deeper involvement in whatever they do and have a tendency to perceive these activities as worth doing. Persons strong in commitment have a strong sense of purpose and direction and do not easily give up under pressure. Commitment is reflected in the ability to feel activity involved with others and a belief in the truth, value and importance of one's self and one's experience (Huang & Wagnitd, 1995; Tartasky, 1993). Adverse situations are ultimately seen as meaningful and interesting (Maddi & Kobasa, 1985).

154

Control- They have a tendency to feel and act in an influential manner in the face of varied contingencies of life. They feel both capable and empowered to achieve desired outcomes (Kobasa, 1979).They act as they are influential in contingencies of life, events are perceived as a natural outgrowth to the individuals actions and not as unexpected experiences(Kobasa et al., 1982).

Challenge- Hardy people tend to perceive changes as a challenge, for them anticipation of changes are interesting incentives to growth rather than threat to security. Challenge reflects the belief that change is not a threat to personal security, but an opportunity for personal development and growth (Kobasa & Maddi, 1984). Hardiness reduces unhealthy effects of stress in two ways: (1) it improves health by acting as a buffer to stressful life events (Kobasa & Puccetti, 1983) and (2) it directly reduces the strain by decreasing the use of unsuccessful coping strategies (Kobasa et al., 1982).

SELF-ESTEEM

Self-esteem refers to an individual's sense of his or her value or worth, or the extent to which a person values, approves of, appreciates, prizes or likes him or herself. The most broad and frequently cited definition of self esteem is by Rosenberg (1965), who described it as a favorable or unfavorable attitude towards the self. Self esteem is generally considered the evaluative component of the self concept, a broader representation of the self that includes cognitive and behavioral aspects as well as evaluative or affective ones. While the construct is most often used to refer to a global sense of self worth, narrower concepts such as self confidence or body esteem are used to imply a sense of self esteem in more specific domains. It is also widely assumed that self esteem functions as a trait, that is, it is stable across time within individuals (Blascovich & Tomaka, 1991).

Different people have different levels of self esteem. Some people think they are wonderful while others think they are worthless. People with drugs or alcohol problems often have low self esteem. They judge themselves negatively- not just for their addiction but also for other parts of their behavior or their personality. Such negativity about themselves would influence their capability in dealing with life or coping with life events. So they might then turn to alcohol to deal with those feelings, if only temporarily. From there they may come to rely or depend on them.

Then of course the habitual use of substance / alcohol may further damage self esteem and reinforce those negative beliefs, which may lead to alcohol dependence/drug dependence. Thus self esteem may play a key role in maintaining the vicious circle around use of different levels of alcohol.

LEARNED HELPLESSNESS

The model of learned helplessness given by Seligman(1973) describes states of helplessness that exist in humans who have experienced numerous failures (either real or perceived).The individual abandons any further attempts toward success. Seligman theorized that learned helplessness predisposes individuals to depression by imposing a feeling of lack of control over their life situations (McKinney & Moran, 1982). It has been empirically proven that negative expectations about the effectiveness of one's own efforts in bringing about the control over one's own environment leads to passivity and diminished initiation of responses (Abrahmson, Seligman & Teasdale, 1978). The term learned helplessness describes an organism's reaction when it is faced with important events that cannot be altered by its voluntary responses. Learned helplessness is both a behavioral state and a personality trait of one who believes that control has been lost over the reinforcers in the environment. These negative expectations lead to helplessness, passivity and an inability to assert oneself.

In both animals and humans, alcohol consumption and learned helplessness are clearly related but alcohol use typically increases following the trauma. It is found in a study with rats very modest increases in alcohol consumption on days when shocks were administered but dramatic increases in alcohol on subsequent days (Volpicelli, et al., 1990). It is noted that even among social drinkers, alcohol consumption increases following the traumatic event but not during.

So, feelings of learned helplessness might influence the individual's use/abuse of alcohol in the face of stressful situations. In this condition the individual assumes that he cannot control the situations or environment and simply stops trying to make things better and starts taking substance/alcohol to control the situations. Further the learned helplessness may pre dispose him towards dependence rather than controlled drinking.

OBJECTIVES

5)   To determine the relationship between hardiness and different levels of alcohol use.

6)   To determine the relationship between self-esteem and different levels of alcohol use.

7)   To determine relationship between learned helplessness and different levels of alcohol use.

8)   To determine relative contribution of hardiness, self esteem and learned helplessness on different levels of alcohol use.

HYPOTHESES

9) Increased level of alcohol use will be negatively related to Hardiness and its dimensions i.e. commitment, Challenge and Control.

10)   Increased level of alcohol use will be negatively related to self-esteem.

11)   Increased level of alcohol use will be positively related to learned helplessness.

12)   There will be significant difference between the three groups Social Drinkers, Problem Drinkers and Alcohol Dependents in

relation to Commitment, Challenge and Control.

13) There will be significant difference between the three groups Social Drinkers, Problem Drinkers and Alcohol Dependents in relation to Hardiness.

14) There will be significant difference between the three groups Social Drinkers, Problem Drinkers and Alcohol Dependents in relation to Self-esteem.

15) There will be significant difference between the three groups Social Drinkers, Problem Drinkers and Alcohol Dependents in relation to Learned Helplessness.

16) Hardiness, self-esteem & learned helplessness will significantly contribute to increase level of alcohol use.

TOOLS

1 Short Alcohol Dependence Data questionnaire (SADD; Raistrick, Dunbar, &Davidson, 1983). This measure is a 15-item measure that assesses the range of current state alcohol dependence (i.e., behavioral, subjective, and psychobiological changes associated with alcohol dependence). Items were answered by checking off one of the following and scored as follows: never= 0, sometimes=1, often= 2, or nearly always= 3. A 45 is the maximum possible score. Concurrent validity was demonstrated by the SADD's association with the Severity of Alcohol Dependence Questionnaire (SADQ; Stockwell et. al., 1979) of rho=.83, p> .01 (Davidson & Raistrick, 1986). The SADD has evidence of good split-half reliability ($r= .87$; Raistrick, Dunbar, & Davidson, 1983).

2 Hardiness Scale: To measure the hardiness level of subjects Psychological Hardiness Scale (Kobasa & Kahn, 1982) was used. The scale consists of 12 items positively and negatively keyed covering the important dimensions of hardiness as commitment, control and challenge. The scale was administered to the subjects after translating into Punjabi. Scoring was done in accordance to the manual of the scale. The reliability coefficiant of the translated scale was found to be 0.628 by the investigator. The validity of the scale was also found to be 0.543.

3 Self-esteem Inventories- Adult Form, The scale developed by Coopersmith's (1981) it is uni-dimensional scale which measures the self-esteem level. This form is used with persons aged 16 and above. It consists of 25 items which are to be answered "like me or unlike me". It has both positive and negative items to be answered. Maximum score is 100. High score corresponds to high self-esteem. The author reported its internal consistency reliability (determined by Kuder-Richerdson formula) 0.81 and 0.86. Test-retest reliability reported by author to be 0.88 and 0.70 respectively.

4 Learned Helplessness Scale: (Dhar, U., Kohli, S., & Dhar, S.,1987). To measure the learned helplessness of subjects the learned helplessness scale was used. This scale consists of 15-items. All items have to be answered in positive, negative and uncertain, and that no

160

statement is to be left out right item was scored as 3, wrong 1 and uncertain as 2. These are designed to have differences in individual reactions to various situations. The scale was administered to the subjects individually as the subjects were not available in groups. Scoring was done as per the manual. The reliability of the scale was determined by two methods (i) The dependability coefficient (Test-Retest) on a sample of 100 subjects is 0.77.(ii) The split half reliability coefficient on a sample of 100 subjects is 0.46 significant at 0.1 level. In order to determine validity from the coefficient of reliability (Garret, 1971), the reliability index was calculated indicated high validity.

SAMPLE

The final sample of the study consisted of 300 adult males. They were in the age group of 25-45 years. This sample was selected out of a larger sample of 500 subjects, so as to have equal numbers of Social Drinkers, Problem Drinkers and Alcohol Dependents belonging to rural and urban areas of Punjab.

STATISTICAL ANALYSIS

Pearson's correlation was worked out to see the relationship of Hardiness, Self-esteem and Learned Helplessness with different levels of Alcohol use. One-way ANOVA was carried out to see the difference between the three groups Social Drinkers, Problem Drinkers and Alcohol Dependents. 't' ratio were also calculated to check the comparision of the three groups. To check the relative contribution of hardiness, self esteem and learned helplessness on different levels of alcohol use step-wise regression analysis was conducted.

MAIN FINDINGS OF THE STUDY

- Significant negative relation was found between increased level of alcohol use and Hardiness as a whole for three groups but for Problem Drinkers Commitment and Control dimension was not related significantly. In Social Drinkers and Alcohol Dependents the relationship existed across all dimensions of Hardiness.

- Increased level of alcohol use was found significantly negatively related to self-esteem for Social Drinkers and Alcohol Dependents but not for Problem Drinkers; although in the latter the relationship was negative in nature.

- Significant positive relation was found between increased level of alcohol use and Learned Helplessness for Alcohol Dependents but this positive relationship was not significant for Social Drinkers and Problem Drinkers.

- Significant difference was found between the three groups in relation to Hardiness. But no significant difference was found between the three groups in relation to Commitment.

- In relation to Challenge significant difference was found between Social Drinkers and Problem Drinkers, Social Drinkers and Alcohol Dependents and no significant difference was found between Problem Drinkers and Alcohol Dependents.

- Control dimension showed significant difference between the three groups. Although Alcohol Dependents showed less score on Control than Social Drinkers and Problem Drinkers.

- Self-esteem of Alcohol Dependents was found significantly low as compared to Social Drinkers and Problem Drinkers. Yet significant difference was found between the three groups in relation to Self-esteem.

- Significant difference was found between the three groups in relation to Learned Helplessness. But Learned Helplessness of Alcohol Dependents was found significantly more as compared to Social Drinkers and Problem Drinkers.

- Hardiness, Self-esteem & Learned Helplessness contributed significantly for Social Drinkers whereas did not contribute significantly to increased level of alcohol use for Problem Drinkers and Alcohol Dependents.

CPSIA information can be obtained
at www.ICGtesting.com
Printed in the USA
LVHW112040270323
742731LV00020BA/608